The Power of Connection

The Power *of* Connection

Jane S. Hall

IPBOOKS.net
International Psychoanalytic Books

International Psychoanalytic Books (IPBooks)
New York • http://www.IPBooks.net

The Power of Connection
Published by IPBooks, Queens, NY
Online at: www.IPBooks.net

Copyright © 2022 Jane S. Hall

All rights reserved. This book may not be reproduced, transmitted, or stored, in whole or in part by any means, including graphic, electronic, or mechanical without the express permission of the author and/or publisher, except in the case of brief quotations embodied in critical articles and reviews.

ISBN: 978-1-956864-39-7

Dedication

For all those who have summoned the curiosity and courage to take the journey inside.

Contents

Preface

Psychoanalysis is in essence a cure through love.
—Sigmund Freud

"The real drive to understand the self, though, comes not from the need to develop treatments, but from a more deep-seated urge that we all share: the desire to understand ourselves. Once self-awareness emerged through evolution, it was inevitable that an organism would ask, 'Who am I?' Across vast stretches of inhospitable space and immeasurable time, there suddenly emerged a person called Me or I. Where does this person come from? Why here? Why now? You, who are made of star-dust, are now standing on a cliff, gazing at the starlit sky pondering your own origins and your place in the cosmos."
— V.S. Ramachandran

The ideas expressed in the following pages are inspired by my patients, my supervisees and their patients, my students, and the vast psychoanalytic literature beginning with Freud and including our most contemporary thinkers.

When I was a student—no computers or PEP-CD Rom—I would spend hours in the New School Library reading the assigned articles. Back then, due to an as yet unanalyzed rebelliousness combined with a deep curiosity, I would read almost all the other articles in the bound volumes, saving the assigned ones for last. In other words I wandered through the fields "picking up lots of forget-me-nots" that I stored away for later use.

I mention, with immense gratitude, the ideas of the following authors whose contributions, some of them well researched, have made a deep impression: Joseph Sandler, Norman Doidge, Rona Knight, Jaak Pankseep, W.R.D. Fairbairn, Ed Tronick, Ella Sharpe, Bernard Berliner, and Leonard Shengold. Actually, there are many others too numerous to mention.

My imagined readers are the clinicians who assist us in exploring who we are, who we would like to be, and what stands in the way; and also those who are curious about depth psychotherapy. It is quite amazing that the general public persists in stigmatizing psychoanalytic exploration of the mind that today includes research from neuroscience, affect theory, and psychological development.

The idea of saying anything that comes into one's mind to interested, non-judgmental others who immerse themselves in analytic thought but are open to the uniqueness of the individual, and who will listen for as long as it takes, is a life enhancing opportunity leading to relief of pain and to new choices. For some, it is life-saving. Being listened to by a respectful and benevolently curious other serves as a catalyst to continued growth and development.

The following essays and riffs will hopefully illustrate my particular slant on depth psychotherapy with an emphasis on the developmental tasks that were once considered age limited but are now seen as going on throughout life. The impressive scientific research done by Rona Knight (2021) tells us to update much of what we have learned from Freud, Klein, and even Winnicott. Knight said:

> *"The old Freudian and Kleinian developmental theories and language do not serve us well when we think about development—not with our patients, not in our understanding of the human condition and certainly not in our interactions with the world outside psychoanalysis."*

She goes on to suggest that we change the way we categorize developmental phases and that we use the more up to date developmental theory of "nonlinear dynamic systems theory"... that

> *"incorporates biology, cognition, the family, the environment and the current culture into the development of a person's internal world of self and other, of conflict and defense, and of ways of coping with external events that can be both rigid and flexible."*

The psychoanalytic work that I propose in these essays takes place on a level playing field with the analyst and analysand, otherwise known as the dyad, working as partners towards figuring out new solutions to problems that have roots in childhood, and that usually involve derailed development. My premise is that once development gets back on track, the pain of failure and loss diminishes allowing the resumption of growth. I replace *interpretations* with explanations created during the dyad's conversations over time. This contemporary dyad does not look to linger in the transference longer than necessary, but uses it as clues to discover where development got stuck. This partnership in and of itself provides new experiences, including the analyst as new object, that are internalized. My basic knowledge of neuroscience and brain neural pathways tells me that due to the plasticity of our brains, we can actually change the way we think.

However, I am also concerned that with all these theories we run the risk of ignoring the uniqueness of the individuals who seek therapy to conquer their demons—to improve their lives—and to overcome whatever stands in the way of moving forward. Over the years I have worked with many people who were, to varying degrees, emotionally abused and neglected in childhood causing them ongoing strain trauma. As adults their ability to function at work and even socially often hid an underlying craving for love and an inability to form satisfying relationships. The connection between patient and therapist proves to be essential in diminishing this pain by getting development back on track.

Too many of our current theories are built using groups of people who are given spurious diagnoses that tend to lead the clinician away from recognizing uniqueness and individuality. My hope is to encourage the depth therapist to reevaluate certain 'received wisdom,' in order to incorporate what recent research is providing, and to think creatively based on new discoveries, always with the unique individual in mind.

These essays and riffs go beyond what I learned at a classical institute and also from what the establishment considers psychoanalysis. But analysis of the psyche takes many forms. I question some of our long held practices like the *rule* of free associations followed by interpretation of an infantile neurosis by a neutral, abstinent, listener. Instead, I suggest a cooperative venture with the patient and analyst as co-workers facing problems by sharing thoughts and ideas. Substituting interpretation with explanation means valuing conversation that includes free talk along with focused attention. Such an approach improves ego functioning and softens the harsh superego. Motives and fears that one has been unaware of, and unconscious fantasies that we believe affect us, emerge, and are explored. Dare I call this psychoanalysis? Well, it is analysis of the psyche but rather than get bogged down in what to call it, I offer these ideas to help those patients who can benefit. I think "psychoanalysis" has lost its way if it cannot be flexible.

Many have benefitted from psychoanalytic work but I know too many who have been disappointed, even injured. Friends and colleagues who were self-motivated along with people who are required to undertake analysis in order to become analysts have been damaged. And while I believe that anyone who decides to become a depth therapist will have experienced their own analysis, this must be their choice and not a requirement, just as the choice of analyst must be a personal one. These essays and riffs are my attempt to examine conformity and to encourage new ideas, without saying "That's Not Analysis."

But just what is analysis? Freud (1914) wrote:

> *It may thus be said that the theory of psychoanalysis is an attempt to account for two striking and unexpected facts of observation which emerge whenever an attempt is made to trace the symptoms of a neurotic back to their sources in his past life: the facts of transference and resistance. Any line of investigation which recognizes these two facts and takes them as the starting point of its work may call itself psychoanalysis though it arrives at results other than my own.* (SE: 1914d, pg. 16)

Somehow these recommendations, as Freud carefully called them, were calcified into rules propagated by the Board of Professional Standards at the American Psychoanalytic Association and they spread to other institutes. The results did great harm to the field and to the patients who were deprived of all that analysis had to offer.

Bhaskar Sripada's (2013) definition is preferred by me:

> *Analysis is an insightful and corrective balm on man's suffering. Any analyst's ability to help a patient is influenced by the degree to which the analyst feels free to employ his own personality in the pursuit of the treatment. Many of our current problems can be remedied by remembering and accepting Freud's original and essential definition of psychoanalysis but adapting it on the basis of every individual analysts's freedom and for the good of the patient.*

Clinging to the past does not serve us well unless one is an antique collector.

I decided to collect these essays and riffs, written over the past ten years, some quite recently, to share my learning curve and to see where I stand now that I dedicate my time to supervising, consulting, and teaching, nationally and internationally, after almost five decades of involvement in psychoanalytic work. Hopefully, *The Power of Connection* will be as helpful as *Deepening the Treatment*. I consider it a sequel.

The following pages are meant to praise psychoanalytic thinkers and researchers for providing models of the mind and also for suggesting clinical approaches. The book is also a tribute to the clinicians who dedicate their professional lives to listening to their patients with benevolent curiosity (Sharpe, 1950) and to those who contribute to our literature and at our meetings, with open minds. The work we clinicians have chosen is honorable, honest, difficult, and fascinating. It requires patience and a special kind of love. Immersion in analytic thought sustains us but must not limit our creativity. Connecting with each unique patient is a challenge that requires ingenuity.

Rather than fit the patient into a theory, I suggest that each unique dyad write their own theory—an idea my first supervisor proposed (Nass, 1975).

My plea is for open-mindedness, respect for the unique human being, and the realization that there is always more to learn. Each of us has something of value to offer and our questions are actually more valuable than answers.

Again, dare I call this psychoanalysis?

Yes.

Introduction and Philosophy

The Power of Connection

The analyst's feeling of certainty is often tied to the idea that there exists a proper "analytic technique" derived from ideas passed down from one generation of analysts to the next (which may be codified by particular "schools" of analytic thinking). By contrast, think of "analytic style" as one's own personal creation that is loosely based on existing principles of analytic practice, but more importantly is a living process that has its origins in the personality and experience of the analyst.

— Ogden (2007)

Too many writers cannot come to terms with the ways in which the past, like the future, is dark. There is so much we don't know, and to write truthfully about a life, your own or your mother's, or a celebrated figure's, an event, a crisis, another culture is to engage repeatedly with those patches of darkness, those nights of history, those places of unknowing. They tell us that there are limits to knowledge, that there are essential mysteries, starting with the notion that we know just what someone thought or felt in the absence of exact information.

— Rebecca Solnit

You know I went to school
And I'm nobody's fool
That is to say until I met you!
I know a little bit about a lot o' things
But I don't know enough about you
— Peggy Lee

What follows is offered with humility during a worrisome time—a time with strains of Covid haunting the world, a time of global warming with its tragic effects, a time of fighting prejudice, of increasing gun violence, and a time of serious division in America that threatens democracy. How we react, adjust, protest, and survive depends a lot on how we use our energy effectively. Mental health must be a priority.

This collection is for anyone who is curious about how one psychoanalyst's thoughts have evolved after five decades in the field. Thanks to my own meandering journeys, my own on-going self-analysis, and thanks to my patients, to those I supervise and teach, and to my colleagues, I feel freer and more curious every day, and the design of this book reflects that. Longer essays, shorter riffs and even a poem will hopefully provide food for thought. After all these years I am increasingly interested in how the brain and the mind are related and how depth therapy figures in. I am most interested in how a dyad connects and what that connection can accomplish.

I must say up front that some of these ideas will seem old-hat to many, and to some they will sound un-psychoanalytic, so my hope is for open-minded consideration. I respect many theories of technique because we are all unique and because we are exploring unchartered territory with each patient. My slant is just that: a slant. It is a perspective that I offer based on my work with patients, many of whom have experienced degrees of childhood strain trauma that interfered with optimal development. It is a perspective that is influenced by a basic knowledge about neural pathways in the brain; how the stress hormone cortisol, and the love hormone oxytocin affect the brain's development (Doidge, 2007); and by new research findings about development (Knight, 2021).

I have always believed that the emergence of negative transference and the rage upon which it is based needs expression, but the question is: how much and for how long. How the dyad deals with it, and what they learn from its expression, is one of the most important questions in our work because an ongoing expression of primitive rage can wear both parties down and may engrave an original trauma more deeply in the brain's neural pathways. Of course, the answers depend on the unique patient's history, but when development has been derailed, and I believe this happens more often than we recognize or realize, we must find ways to get it back on track. This includes learning about our earliest days which is sometimes possible but most times not, along with our history of relationships. Think in terms of knitting a sweater. Dropped stitches in the beginning can be easily overlooked when the sweater is finished unless you look carefully. But will the sweater hold its shape over time? Unfinished or incomplete developmental tasks can be hard to spot in the adult patient, especially in the beginning stages of analytic treatment, but when impasse threatens or progress is stalled due to a patient's difficulty with reality, I have found that solid enough differentiation between self and object and incomplete separation and individuation need attention. So many things too numerous to list, including genetic disposition, how mother and baby match, illness, and early loss to name just a few, impinge upon how the child takes in and processes its surrounds. These things are what make us unique.

With this in mind, I am suggesting a level playing field with two people working together, where the analyst shares her strength with her partner until her partner feels increasingly stronger. In other words, I am considering how we redress the damage done by varieties of trauma which affect, to varying degrees, the tasks of differentiation between self and object, the separation-individuation process, and the formation of a self. I think that many patients reach impasses if this is overlooked. We are also faced with the serious dissociation that occurs in patients subjected to severe, ongoing trauma. Purcell (2019) informs us in his moving paper that with

> *"unrepresented experience—something different is needed at the level of "technique": a technical attitude—one of doing things to our patients—must largely be replaced by a way of being with our patients.... being with his analysand in non-meaning as well as in symbolic communication. In being the analyst for traumatized people, technical rules and maneuvers must give way to improvisation and creativity, integral elements of an artistry that must find its place in the analyst's attitude."*

My imaginary reader shares with me the insatiable wish to understand the mysteries of why we are who we are. Having reached a certain age I realize that the more I see and the more I learn, the more I recognize how much more there is to discover. I have gained an increasing appreciation of how very complicated the human mind and brain are and I am in awe of those who dedicate their time and energy to understanding how the mind interacts with the brain, how the outside affects the inside, and how epigenetic change occurs. Psychoanalysis offers the most thorough approach to solving such mysteries, especially when scientific research is acknowledged. Cultivating and keeping an open mind makes almost everything seem possible.

These heretofore unpublished essays and riffs were written over the past ten plus years, some quite recently, and are now the chapters of this book. My focus is on how the connection between two people, known as the dyad, encourages the growth that leads to change. Even our most challenging patients hopefully come to know on some level when someone is listening without criticism. This book is a sequel to *Deepening the Treatment*, and the reader will see that my philosophy has shifted from a more classical view of our work to what I consider a more contemporary one that takes into consideration research in neuroscience, affects, and child development.

How two strangers connect and the importance of that connection is the underlying theme of this book. Conversation connects us, whether in person, on Zoom-like platforms, via email or snail mail, or over the telephone. I think that all the words we use, even in one session or over the entire course of treatment, serve as the glue that bind the dyad together. And sometimes I think that if our hearts are in the right place, it matters not so much what we say to each other but how we say it. Angry words, loving words, fancy words, empty words, lack of words are important yet when all is said and done, neither party in the dyad remembers much of what was said when treatment has ended. What is remembered are the feelings beneath the words and the spontaneous moments of laughter, tears, and of feeling genuinely caring, cared about, and accepted.

About the couch: During analysis there are times when reading a person's facial expression is beneficial for both parties in the dyad. This is particularly important for the patient with an avoidant attachment style where the goal is connecting positively with a new object instead of reinforcing memories of the early, depriving and traumatic objects. When patients repeat the past in the transference instead of using it as a clue to the mystery, such repetition risks reinforcing the original trauma. As a new object relationship is formed by in depth, libidinal connection with the analyst over time, the brain's circuitry changes. The phrase 'use it or lose it' applies here so if you had a bad object relationship with a parent, and then you develop a better one with a new object, the fact that you have a trace of the old one doesn't mean you have to use it (Doidge, 2007).

Our first conversations in life take the form of the cooing and crying of infancy and the way they are responded to. These earliest connections play a major part in determining the bond we form with our mothers/caretakers and serve as a major template for future relationships. There is solid evidence that human beings are inextricably intertwined with one another from the earliest moments of infancy. At birth, the infant appears hard-wired to seek human interaction. Along with words, conversation includes how we communicate with our eyes, our posture, odor, style, our facial expressions, silences, the way we listen, and especially our unconscious vibes. In psychoanalysis the conversation goes on consistently over time in a safe place with a non-judgmental, trustworthy other.

Analysis involves a certain amount of regression, so the couch is helpful for those who have frequent enough sessions. But at times it is useful to read a person's facial expression, particularly with the deprived adult with an avoidant attachment style. I like the idea of a swivel reclining chair for the patient who can then have a choice.

One of the most important things I have learned is that those who have grown up with unavailable, narcissistic, or abusive parents or caretakers have trouble giving and receiving love as adults. We get used to our earliest diets and have great difficulty in digesting new food. We seek out the same restaurants because the food is familiar and familiarity means safety, even when painful. We choose partners who echo the past because feeling safe is a basic need. I see no harm in mentioning this tendency to a patient at an appropriate time.

It is my hope that with these chapters I succeed in connecting with you, the reader, as I talk about my philosophy of clinical work, my experiences with patients, and what I have learned as a clinician, consultant, and teacher.

This collection is meant not only for depth psychotherapists, but also for anyone interested in psychoanalytic ideas. My pronouns switch at random for the sake of brevity and out of respect for gender preferences. I use the word 'patient' out of habit. (A patient is any recipient of health care services that are performed by healthcare professionals.) I would prefer 'learner' or 'adventurer' or 'partner in solving mysteries' but I fear this would sound too futuristic. 'Co-traveler' would be good too because I see psychoanalytic work as a journey taken by two, a meandering journey (Chapter Three).

Why another book? The field is crowded with interesting, scholarly, and useful literature and I'm sure that just about everything has been said, one way or another. Many psychoanalysts are excellent writers who have even contributed fiction, memoir, and poetry. Ted Jacobs, Tom Ogden, Christopher Bollas, Arlene Heyman, Sandra Beuchler, Eugene Mahon, and Kerry Malawista come immediately to mind. Many erudite authors are sometimes more difficult to read but often well worth the effort. My style/voice is direct—no vibrato, just plain and simple. Speaking of voices, I use jazz music in Chapter Ten, On Listening, to encourage the idea of creating something new.

Hopefully, my slant, that has been developing over all these years will be of use. Also, I have been working on these essays and riffs for a long time with the hope that someone will get something from them. The song *"T'ain't What You Do, It's the Way That You Do It"* comes to mind because our voices make us unique. One more reason: psychoanalytic observations and theories have gained sophistication over the years and so have psychoanalytic clinicians. Our methods are now making use of the impressive research in child development and in neuroscience. I want to encourage therapists to fight the lure of *received wisdom* and to allow new findings to stretch their minds.

"*... you work to turn the ghosts that haunt you into ancestors who accompany you. That takes hard work and a lot of love, but it is the way we lessen the burdens our children have to carry... I work to be an ancestor*" said Bruce Springsteen in *Born to Run*. Hans Loewald also spoke of turning ghosts into ancestors. In fact, isn't that what all we clinicians do? Ghost busting is our business.

Freud deserves our deepest respect and appreciation. He will always accompany us but psychoanalytic work has advanced and branched out to serve all kinds of people as I'm sure he would have wanted it to. By the way, Freud was far more relational than many of his followers have acknowledged. He conducted a number of walking analyses, according to Peter Gay in *Freud: A Life for Our* Time. Besides his four hour walk with Gustav Mahler, Freud conducted his first training analysis on Max Eitingon in 1907 through a series of evening walks. Eitingon went on to become president of the International Psychoanalytic Association and created a model of training still used today. I sometimes wonder whether some of our founding fathers and mothers analyzed their sadomasochistic tendencies with such short analyses; and how their influence affects us in today's analytic world.

Freud's phallocentric, oedipal focus has been challenged by Breger (2009), Barron (1991) Simon (1991), and Holtzman & Kulish (2000) among others. The research on attachment and the separation-individuation tasks of development featuring both the maternal and paternal influences has changed the phallocentric focus.

As I look at today's world with so many adamant believers in bizarre conspiracies, along with the rampant misogyny finally being brought to justice thanks to the "me too" movement, I believe that early childhood anxieties and the transmission of trauma play a large part. Paranoia can be seen as one result of early and on going anxiety. It has always been a part of society but social media fans its flames. With society's pressures increasing, many parents are unable to provide the safety and security that children need in order to differentiate and to individuate. Parents cannot help but pass on their own fears and anxiety to their children who often fail to develop a secure sense of self. This is not new, but the research is now available proving that children thrive under certain conditions. And even when parents are caring and available, things can go radically wrong due to certain social media platforms.

My ideas about leveling the playing field and distancing our techniques from the medical model harken back to when psychoanalysis came to America in 1911 as a medical sub-specialty. The analyst as a medical doctor, all too often took on the persona of a blank screen that was meant to help the patient develop a transference neurosis (an emotional relationship with the analyst based on childhood relationships). This has been referred to as classical or orthodox psychoanalysis. The results of a law suit claiming restraint of trade, and settled in 1989, changed the profession by allowing psychologists, social workers, and qualified others to join the ranks by studying at the American Psychoanalytic training institutes. However, their teachers were M.D.s whose model featured diagnosis, prognosis, and cure. This model heavily influenced the field in America. I join many who question seeing the analyst in the role of the physician administering a treatment based upon a judgment of psychopathology which determines analyzability. The infantilization of the patient (and of the student in training) has seriously harmed this field. Even the word 'training' instead of education illustrates a less than humanistic attitude. So-called 'lay analysts' were ignored by the medical establishment despite Freud's impassioned plea (1926). Theodore Reik, a non-M.D., began his own independent institute, the National Psychological Association for Psychoanalysis dedicated to teaching non-physicians. Others soon followed suit.

The view I take is a continuation of Leo Stone's (1954) humanistic approach. I am most impressed by Sandor Ferenczi who envisioned the analysand as a co-participant in the dyad. I appreciate and support the emphasis on empathic reciprocity during the therapeutic encounter which is an important contribution from the evolution of the intersubjective/relational school of psychoanalysis. Both parties in the dyad must be free to share experiences when appropriate, in contrast to the abstinent/blank screen approach advocated by the orthodox analysts. I see the dyad as a partnership that leaves room for the evolving transferences to be understood and adjusted thus allowing for something new. Freud's followers in Berlin led by Max Eitingon did him a disservice by bringing an authoritarian approach to both students and patients.

I learned, practiced, and appreciate many ideas espoused by the classical model but differ with its *analyst as blank screen* approach because it deprives patients of forming a new human connection that I find indispensable to growth. The medical model initially practiced in America could not help but affect how the analyst and patient viewed each other and this patient/doctor image, understandable as it may be in other circumstances, is what I suggest needs adjusting. I propose in these essays and riffs a basic shift in the way many (not all) psychoanalysts still work with patients. The mindset of a doctor implies a top-down, authoritarian slant and our society bows to this approach. We want a doctor to cure us and here is where I offer a different point of view. The idea of working together to get development back on track is very different from a doctor curing a patient by interpreting her free associations. It is different because as patients resume development it is they who do what is necessary to move forward in life. I see the therapist as facilitating development. Along these lines I propose that explanation and conversation take the place of interpretation. Yes, the analyst shares what she hears but not as a pronouncement.

The shift that I envision suggests a level playing field where two people view problems together—as co-workers. This does not preclude transference explanations; we all see the present influenced by past experience. But both partners use their transference vision in the service of going beyond. This approach is especially applicable to those whose early years were unsteady and traumatic. What I am proposing is that both parties in the dyad discuss possible ways of understanding the clues presented by the patient, rather than setting up the analyst as the authoritative interpreter—the one with the answers. The attitude that includes discussion in and of itself builds the patient's ego or sense of agency. This idea will not be new to many depth therapists who have not undergone classical analytic training that focuses on analysis of defense.

I am not concerned here with talking about theories, such as Intersubjective or Self-psychology or the structural versus the topographic, and so forth, and I don't dwell on differentiating psychoanalysis and psychoanalytic psychotherapy, a topic that has plagued this field for too many years. Beneath the theories lay the therapist's stance. Does she see disease/illness/pathology, or does she think in terms of derailed development and once necessary adaptations that are no longer useful or necessary? How a clinician views a patient's difficulties is what I suggest needs serious rethinking. Instead of focusing on what's *wrong* exclusively, I suggest seeing what's right. We all adapt as best we can to the cards we've been dealt in childhood so why call this pathology? Early adaptations have been life saving if you think about it—but like childhood shoes, we outgrow them. The right to have new shoes is what therapists hope to instill. Benevolent curiosity (Sharpe, 1950) is the bedrock of the method I am presenting. Her words:

> *"The urgency to reform, correct, or make different motivates the task of a reformer or educator, the urgency to cure motivates the physician, but free to range over every field of human experience and activity, free to recognize every unconscious impulse, with only one urgency, namely, a desire to know more, and still more. When we react to something that causes us to think 'I cannot understand how a person can think or behave like that' curiosity has ceased to be benevolent."*

Thanks to the research on child development (Knight, 2021; Tronick, 2001) and the discovery of the brain's plasticity, the psychoanalyst's palette is filled with more colors than our forefathers and mothers had available. I propose adding to or even replacing Freud's phallocentric, oedipal model with a developmental model, featuring the quality of the bond between the infant and its caretakers, the separation-individuation phase with it's task of differentiating self from object, as central. To put it plainly: too many have not fully realized that there are 'others' who think differently, and so are unable to respect diversity. I see the analytic goal as getting derailed development back on track. For those who find Mahler's model limited, I suggest Ed Tronick's (2001) Dyadic Expansion of Consciousness hypothesis. But both theories center on the child's early connection to the mothering figure. Thanks to Rona Knight's research we have learned that development continues throughout life and is not limited to specific ages.

My extensive experience with patients who suffered strain trauma in childhood has shaped many of the ideas in this book. Although I respect and consider the many theories available, I am committed to greeting each patient as unique. Our tendency to apply a diagnosis and then a theory to an individual limits what we see. The unique patient creates the theory (Nass, 1975).

Technique has changed gradually in that its elements, such as furniture and frequency, are no longer written in stone. But many training institutes guided by the Eitingon model still require these artifacts. Why do we cling to them? Yes, using the couch can be helpful but making its use a requirement is insensitive to the unique individual.

This book takes issue with the analyst as mostly silent interpreter of the patient's free associations. I picture two people facing the problems together as detectives solving mysteries? (See Lois in Chapter Three: Self-Murder.) This stance requires respect and benevolent curiosity. Over time the dyad develops a relationship that includes transference love, real love, hatred, and everything in between. Transferences serve as clues. When patients see the others in their lives only in terms of past relationships, their vision needs adjustment. The dyad works together to broaden their view. I must add that I respect the analyst's silence as well. Our patient's must have the opportunity to see where their minds go—so I hope for a flexible approach with the unique patient in mind. A rhythm evolves that accelerates at times and that slows at other times. No metronomes are required.

In essence, I propose that two people share the job of looking into how the past affects the present, with the resumption of development being the goal. The feelings and fantasies (conscious and unconscious) experienced by both parties are explored. One partner may hold the other's anxiety until it diminishes due to the connection that develops. Most of what goes on is unconscious and when enactments that are always happening become evident, the unconscious message is exposed. This exposure releases us from an action mode thus allowing insight. Tronick (1998) suggests that there are dyadic states of consciousness that develop between patient and therapist that he calls 'something more'—and that change is due to these new and unique dyadic states. Purcell (2019) speaks about "a way of being."

Anxiety diminishes when criticism is not involved. In Chapter Nine: "How Long," Lisa's constant tears in the beginning phase of analysis may have been expressing her fear of criticism. Love, not often enough mentioned in our literature, grows out of respect and serves to cushion the discomfort involved in negotiating separation and individuation. Benevolent curiosity is part of love.

We need the new discoveries about the brain and mind. Norman Doidge's message in *The Brain That Changes Itself*, is that during analytic work we choose different neural pathways when the old ones lead to trouble—a bold idea based on the evidence of the brain's plasticity. See Chapter One of his book where he describes the stroke victim's recovery and what the brain autopsy showed after a long and productive life.

I have seen classical analysis help some people but a combination of methods can be useful depending on the unique dyad. The analyst must feel free to titrate the treatment with the unique patient in mind while still calling the treatment psychoanalysis if she so wishes. I believe many of us already feel this freedom so this is meant for those who have felt intimidated by their 'training.' What I suggest is partially based on my own personal experiences, one with an authoritarian training analyst followed by a vastly different personal analysis with a highly respected and revered analyst who refused the title on principle. These experiences helped shape the ideas in these essays.

My major focus is the therapist's slant, attitude, and manner—a manner that is based on respect, a special kind of love, and benevolent curiosity, all three allowing us to experience the patient as unique.

Short riffs and longer essays and even a poem (though by no means am I a poet) express some of what I've learned. Neither text book nor memoir—I present my personal slant on the journey including what I've learned from my experience . While doing research I was floored by the richness of our literature. The plethora of books and articles about psychoanalytic work can only mean that we are forever searching for and sharing ideas. And why not? The human mind is extremely complex, as is the brain and its outposts. Both deserve all the attention we can muster. There is no one way of thinking that captures its mysteries which relates to my feelings about the disadvantages and harm involved in measurement. The way we use the new discoveries mentioned above surely matters just as much as the evidence itself. Ed Tronick and Marjorie Beeghly (2011) speak of an instinct or drive towards *making meaning* that we are all born with and this makes perfect sense to me. There is so much to learn and see and experience. And sometimes, depending on how we use it, all our knowledge can actually impede us and even obscure what our partner is telling us.

Our most famous fictional detective, Sherlock Holmes, says as much in this story:

> *Holmes and Watson are on a camping trip. In the middle of the night Holmes wakes up and gives Dr. Watson a nudge. "Watson" he says, "look up... and tell me what you see." "I see millions of stars, Holmes," says Watson. "And what do you conclude from that, Watson?" Watson thinks for a moment. "Well," he says, "astronomically, it tells me that there are millions of galaxies and potentially billions of planets. Astrologically, I observe that Saturn is in Leo. Horologically, I deduce that the time is*

> *approximately a quarter past three. Meteorologically, I suspect that we will have a beautiful day tomorrow. Theologically, I see that God is all-powerful, and we are small and insignificant. Uh, what does it tell you, Holmes?" "Watson, you idiot! Someone has stolen our tent!"*

A recent reading in Jaak Pankseep's (2012) work on affects, coupled with understanding more about the intersubjective/relational approach so well articulated by Phillip Bromberg, Lew Aron, Stephen Mitchell, Donnel Stern, Jim Fossage, and so many others, and recognizing the plasticity of the brain have shifted my thinking to a broader comprehension of how we relate to each other and to our patients. Heart to heart communication is what matters most, and it often takes place without words. I repeat, more goes on unconsciously than we can ever know. This is why the therapist's hope is important. Our patient's pick it up subliminally.

I have always shied away from diagnostic categories because I fear boxing people in. They provide some advantages, as Nancy McWilliams (2011) has beautifully shown us, but for many therapists these categories can stand in the way of hope. Nancy says:

> *"Once one has learned to see clinical patterns that have been observed for decades, one can throw away the book and savor individual uniqueness."*

However, my concern is that such patterns can affect what we see and experience. I worry that we are too comfortable experiencing a unique individual as being just another hysteric or borderline or obsessive compulsive described in the DSMs. This may obscure other features and patterns that make discovery of the uniqueness of each individual quite difficult if not impossible. If Copernicus had stayed with the received wisdom that the earth and not the sun was the center of our universe, science would not have advanced. *Received wisdom* can be wrong! My point is that the way people have seen things for decades, directs and clouds our vision. Of course, I realize that what we have learned will always influence us but my plea is to be aware of the tendency to categorize, and to replace that tendency by cultivating an open mind. Hearing a person as a unique individual must come first. If we need a frame of reference how about this: the past determines the present and what cannot be articulated will be enacted or acted out. There is a natural course of development and when it has been compromised it is the dyad's job to clear the way for its resumption. Patients who are uncooperative have reasons!

I have not seen evidence that convinces me of the categories that DSM has devised even though they are compelling, and I *have* seen evidence that these categories tend to narrow our thinking, influence our perception, and leave us spinning our wheels. But most importantly, a label can obscure the uniqueness of each individual patient. So, although there is comfort in categories when used as shorthand, or for insurance companies, I fear that the patient and the therapist may get lost in the label. Boxes are like fences to me and a favorite song of mine is *Don't Fence Me In*. I think in terms of development, so separation-individuation and its sub-phases, along with object constancy, and differentiation, are helpful concepts. Did someone get stuck along the way, and if they did, how can they get back on track, I wonder? I use the word "wonder" a lot because it leaves the door open for new ideas and because I hope my co-traveler will wonder too. The arrogance of certainty cuts off so many options.

Phillip Bromberg's (1996) work with self-states makes great sense to me as does a favorite book by a non-analyst psychologist *Stranger in the Mirror: the scientific search of the self*, by Robert V. Levine (2016). Both authors write from different backgrounds but come to similar conclusions: we have many self-states that are not problematic. One is not using the same self-state when facing an emergency as when learning a subject in school or when making love. In fact, what we deem pathology was once adaptive. If we see the adaptive aspects of defensive character structure, our ability to relate to our patients is enhanced. People often forget to think "What's right with you?" Seeing the glass half full helps me. I have said to a patient something like: *"Hiding from the truth (avoidance or denial) was helpful when you were a child but now it holds you back. It's like trying to walk in shoes you have outgrown. They helped then but now they pinch making it hard to move ahead."*

But, you will say, what about the truly impossible patient, the patient who is hostile to the whole idea of therapy. Chapter One, Let's Fall in Love, discusses this dilemma. Bottom line, it is up to the therapist to find creative ways to respond. And sometimes treatment just doesn't get to first base. We do strike out. We are human.

Therapists, like their patients, like to feel safe, and because the familiar is safe, we often cling to it. What we learn in the psychoanalytic institute is difficult to forget. It took me many years to move beyond what I learned in the 1970s and 1980s. I question the set up of our learning institutes. Just as each patient is unique, so is each student and I hope that can be taken into account. Tailoring our knowledge to the individual is an art that must be nurtured. Each dyad creates something unique. So when I said in the beginning of this introduction that nothing is new, I also think everything is new when you expand your vision. I recently discovered David Eagleman and I highly recommend his Ted Talk.

Readers who are dissatisfied, in pain, or curious about psychoanalytic work may be inspired to take a journey inward with an experienced companion. I know of no other journey that is more fulfilling. Chapter Three describes our work as a meandering journey, which will hopefully serve as an invitation.

Not many people leap onto our couches or into our chairs, or even understand our method of work, so degrees of explanation are in order, always tailored to the unique patient. Explanations have not been part of classical work and I wonder why. Most analysts prefer interpretation, which tilts the field, putting the analyst on a higher plane. After a certain amount of time in therapy, it is the patient who will come up with ideas that contribute to growth.

People have a right to know something about what they're getting into and the explanations offered and the ways they are offered can determine the outcome of a first meeting and even of a whole analysis. Everyone has stories to tell and the very act of telling them to an attentive listener promotes growth and solves mysteries. Sherlock Holmes also said: "Nothing clears up a case so much as stating it to another person" (Doyle, 1894). This holds true in working psychoanalytically where colleagues often see our blind spots. Enjoy Chapter Eleven on storytelling.

The fact that a person makes an appointment and keeps it indicates strength and courage. If we remember that each dyad is unique, improvisation is natural and intuition guides us. Genuine spontaneity is important. Messiness is allowed when working this way, but the dyad works towards repair. Claudia Gold and Ed Tronick (2020) explore this idea in their book: *The Power of Discord.* This essential aspect of the dyad's work relies on the present, what we refer to as the *here and now* interaction, and it may even take precedence over revisiting the past. It may also include the past as reference point. *"This reminds me of the time when my sister was born and I was supposed to be the big girl all of a sudden,"* said one patient when discussing her experience at a new job. Her memory opened a new door quite naturally, a door that illustrated the past's influence on the present. "*You just sounded like my father*" said another patient leading to memories of a man who died long ago and who had not been mourned.

Psychoanalytic work is filled with stories and I have found that at times the therapist's stories are a useful part of the relationship. We call this *self-disclosure* and it has been frowned upon by classical analysts. Some might even call it a boundary crossing. But, when the analyst has something to share that is appropriate to what's going on, it seems only natural to do so, spontaneously and genuinely. I give an example in the Listening chapter. I think of my meeting with patients as containing both playfulness and heart-to-heart conversations along with my reflective capacity.

The therapist acts as a guide/companion on the trip of exploration. A crucial aspect of this journey is the motivation to inhabit the present, to envision the wished for or dreaded future while visiting the past when it sheds light on both. Exploring all three dimensions helps us understand ourselves without the need to master 'string theory' or 'time travel.' I think that saying *"That reminds me of xyz"* encourages us to use what comes to mind—what we call free association. Instead of making free association a rule, I see everything a patient says as free. And if he decides to withhold something, I assume he will figure out why as we go along. I have said to patients: *"As we meet, there will be things you wish to keep to yourself. When that happens, try thinking about why. What would happen if you just said whatever pops into your head?"* Usually things withheld involve shame or lack of trust and as the bond strengthens, the patient will feel more comfortable sharing what she thinks. Motivation is enhanced by the rapport established—and it is up to the guide to set a tone of benevolent curiosity. Before trusting one's travel companion, a period of assessment and testing occurs and each party uses both their conscious intelligence and their gut feelings to determine whether the trip feels safe enough to embark on together. I talk about this testing in the Chapter Three: Self-Murder.

Developing trust takes varying amounts of time but it is indispensable when traveling. Patients test us, consciously and unconsciously, so the frame is necessary because it guarantees safety.

I think of the dyad's work as a long conversation, or as solving mysteries together. These analogies help me explain what I do.

Struggling to get an idea across can get messy. Ed Tronick points out that Fred Astaire and his partners surely stepped on each other's toes while practicing before their performances. We make mistakes and we recover. In the recovery lies the growth. And when we goof we apologize.

I begin this book with my first experience as a therapist, still in social work school, with Chapter One: Let's Fall In Love. I wrote these chapters with love—for the field, the patients, my colleagues, and those who I supervise and teach. Love does make the world go round, we just have to find it. I would like to see us all more comfortable with the basic love we feel—the libido Martin Bergmann and I spoke about in Chapter Twelve.

I realize that many ideas show up in multiple chapters which is why skipping around or reading at your leisure is okay.

CHAPTER 1

LET'S FALL IN LOVE

Love cures people—both the ones who give it and the ones who receive it.
— Karl A. Menninger

Love does not consist in gazing at each other, but in looking outward together in the same direction.
— Antoine de Saint-Exupery

This chapter is dedicated to the late Ella Freeman Sharpe whose paper "The Analyst" introduced me to the concept of benevolent curiosity and to the late Leonard Shengold who was not afraid to speak of love's place in psychoanalytic work.

Every working day, those of us who do psychoanalytic work are privileged, challenged, and expected to experience with our patients degrees of every common human feeling from grief to joy, from sadness to elation, and from cooperation to antagonism. For most of us, this work is a calling. Answering that calling is my topic. I was troubled growing up as I imagine many people in this profession have been, so one reason for my dedication to this field is due to the help I got.

Therapists are seen by their patients as heroes, villains, saviors, destroyers, self-objects, and sometimes they are not seen at all. Inwardly, and to varying degrees, therapists feel confident, useless, valuable, loving, angry, bewildered, and enlightened, and sometimes they even fall asleep at the switch. How to keep on going is a question I address here. How do we continue to engage our patients in deepening the treatment—in staying the course,in doing the work—especially in today's world of fast fixes and instant gratification? How do we therapists manage being experienced as compassionate observers, warriors, good and bad parents, and lovers, often at the same time while remaining within the boundaries? How do we tame, sublimate, hold, and use the emotions, both our own and our patients', responsibly and safely? How do we present ourselves as steady, consistent, mostly unruffled, and constant, day after day, year after year? How do we deal with our own reluctance and fear in the day of Covid and global warming? And how do we manage to connect with our patients, many of whom dread and fear any kind of connection?

I ask the reader to join me in pondering these questions.

I am talking about patients with varying degrees of anxiety and depression who come to see us willingly, not so willingly, and even because of some outside requirement. Much of our clinical literature discusses patients who have committed to analytic work—but what about those patients who are on the fringes, who could vastly improve their lives, but who are too frightened and too angry to trust? And what about the patients who seem really stuck and seemingly unable to relate to us? How do we persevere?

Let me introduce Mr. S, my first patient during my social work internship at the Greenwich House Counseling Center in the early 1970s. At that time I was studying psychoanalysis, while completing my MSW. GHCC, funded by the Federal, State and City Governments, specialized in free treatment for those who had drug related problems. Patients came from all walks of life and all socio-economic levels, from professors to prostitutes to fairly average Joes.

I will always remember him—a middle aged, African-American, homeless man, required to come to my clinic by the welfare department.

Mr. S. seemed to have lost everything. If we believe that the past is repeated in the present, we may assume that he experienced losses in childhood, likely never mourned.

First meeting:
Th: (we shake hands) Hi, my name is Jane Hall. How can I help?
Pt: Welfare makes me come—otherwise I'd never be here.
Th: I see. Well, do you think there's anything we can do to make the time worth your while?
Pt: No. I can't see what you can do about my life. I sleep in the subway when I can, lost my family. I freeze in the winter and sweat in the summer. What the hell can you do about that?

Th: I see what you mean. Well, I can listen to you—sometimes that helps.
Pt: Helps what?
Th: Talking is a way of connecting—and people do need to connect to someone for the sake of their health.
Pt: You're a white chick—have nice clothes, a job, probably a family—how can my talking to you have any meaning?
Th: I guess you won't know unless you give it a try.
Pt: I been to jail.
Th: What was it like?
Pt: Don't you want to know why? What I got locked up for?
Th: If you want to tell me.
Pt: I can't. You would hate me if I told.
Th: But that's not why I'm here. My job is to listen to you, not to judge you. You do that yourself it seems.
Pt: What do you mean..
Th: Well, you think I'd hate you. Why is that?
Pt. What I did was bad. I stole.
Th: You must have had a reason.
Pt: I wanted money to get high—to get drugs.
Th: Did drugs make you feel better?

During this meeting I remember feeling inept, concerned, curious, and challenged. Mr. S was a human being in distress. Making occasional eye contact, worrying that I would hate him, and annoyed to be sitting in this clinic. *He answered:*

Pt: Heroin was a way out—made me feel relaxed and soft. No hatred, no worry, just peaceful and warm (something changed as he remembered).

Th: It's no wonder you liked that feeling. It must be so hard to face the reality you described.
Pt: Yeah—and I feel lousy without heroin.
Th: What was it like before you discovered drugs?
Pt: Don't like to go there—always trouble. Grew up in Mississippi...
Slowly, Mr. A began to thaw. But, the time would soon be up.
Th: You've begun to tell me a little about who you are. Will you continue next time? I feel like we've made a start here.
Pt: (pause) Maybe. If I'm still around. Maybe...
I gave him a card with my name and the time of the next appointment.
He accepted it, put it in his wallet and stood up, walking to the door he mumbled thanks.

We can assume that this homeless ex-heroin addict had never shared his pain with an interested human being. Instead he had covered it with drugs. My hope was that by putting his story into words he would find some relief.

Mr. S did return and I invited him to join a small group I was forming.

The clinic required that each therapist run a group. I had no training in group work so I was flying blind. I began by introducing myself to seven men between age fifty and sixty-five who were required to come to GHCC and who had used heroin. Some probably still used occasionally—they called it 'dibbing and dabbing' back then.

We sat in a circle and after each of us said our names, I told some of my story first—that I was studying to be a psychoanalyst. *What's that* one man asked. They were curious so I told them about what I was learning—specifically how one's past can affect the present and how memories are often stored in the unconscious part of the mind. I told them about self-esteem and how liking oneself depends on understanding and figuring out the reasons behind our behavior. I told them about how we all defend ourselves starting in childhood and that these defenses often got in the way as we became adults. When I mentioned that denial was a big defense they asked what I meant. I said most people hide things from themselves like unpleasant feelings and memories.

As we continued talking with me answering their questions I could feel the ice melting and we began to connect. I also told them that I was new at being a therapist but strongly felt that human connection was at the heart of life and that sharing our stories would help us begin to connect. The men slowly started to talk, hesitantly at first but as they listened to each other something began happening. Telling and listening to each other's stories was something they had never experienced. These men had been essentially alone, living out their emptiness and pain by using heroin.

Over a fairly short period of time, maybe six weeks, after listening to each other they gradually began to express interest in each other and their lives gained new purpose and meaning. When one member went to jail the group wrote a letter. Mr. S. admitted that he got himself arrested each year before Thanksgiving so that he could have a turkey dinner and not be alone. Mr. D., another member told him about a church he went to for Thanksgiving dinner and invited him. When another member complained that he was losing his identity as a master thief, Mr. X. offered to teach him to play chess. Mr. C.'s overt paranoia troubled the group but as they reacted to him with concern and a firmness that he could accept he calmed down. Mr. A spoke to him: *"Maybe you just want attention—thinking someone's following you. If you believe someone is out to get you, at least someone knows you exist."* We actually talked about this idea for a whole session. It turned out that the paranoid Mr. C. had been abandoned as a child and grew up in many foster homes. It was true that no one had cared about him and it took him months to realize that the group members did. Their attention was a brand new experience for him.

Sounds magical but I believe that connecting is magical, or at least close to it. More scientifically, when you relate to someone with sincere interest and without judgment a bond based on trust develops. Jaak Pankseep (2012) says it is chemical. If you think about it, our culture is a judgmental one and it doesn't always feel safe. We measure people without even realizing it and that tendency is programed into our brains for good reason. In the cave-man days, according to Mel Brooks' *2000 Year Old Man*, the ability to sense danger was life-saving. He said that the reason people got married was so that one party looked behind, and the other partner looked forward. You can listen to it on YouTube.[1]

Back to the group—we all grew tremendously. Why tell you this story? What is analytically based or relevant here? Well, the first

---

1 https://youtu.be/WWYucilobf *A Two-Thousand-Year-Old Man*

thing about analytic work is getting interested in the "whys" or "reasons" for what we do in life with benevolent curiosity. It opens a new door. But even more important, connecting to a trusted other can be life-saving.

Because it was genuine, my demeanor of openness and respect seemed to mean a lot to the group. I sincerely respected them for showing up each week and for telling their stories. They were used to being criticized, ignored, and looked down on. I was truly curious. I remember saying something like: *"Gentlemen, I have one request and that is to replace all criticism with curiosity."* Perhaps for the first time these men paid and received attention in positive ways. We tend to forget that attention without judgement is what we *all* want—from birth and throughout life. Wondering *why* without judgment is a new experience for most people. Relating with words challenged these men and gave them new ways of seeing things. They learned how to wonder and they learned that being sad was okay and that tears were nothing to be ashamed of. We laughed together at times and a camaraderie developed based on trust. They taught me about basketball and about life on the street. I missed one session when my Dad died and when they asked where I had been I told them. The group asked me about him and it felt good to tell them. The men were caring and I was touched by their sympathy. We grew to like each other and to care about each other. We felt what Shengold (1989) called caritas—a form of love based on concern. One of the hardest things for me was saying goodbye to the group when I left the agency two years after we began. Over fifty years have passed and I think of them to this day.

Celia was another GHCC patient. An ex-heroin addict, she was referred to me when her therapist at the clinic left after a year of weekly therapy. I remember how angry she was about that loss and, as is often the case, she took it out on me.

I learned that when a patient has lost a previous therapist, the new therapist must take the flak in order to move on. Separations revive painful feelings from childhood and facing them helps repair injuries. This applies to all treatments. Adults who experience loss or frequent separation in childhood are not equipped to understand why a loved one goes away and so when a therapist is absent for whatever reason, memories of feeling abandoned surface. The original anxiety and anger is experienced and talking about it helps modify the pain. The opportunity that separations provide are often overlooked by therapists because patient's tend to deny or avoid their feelings but if we listen we can hear clues (Hall, 1998).

Celia was in her late twenties with two children and no father in sight. She was determined to keep her kids and although therapy was a requirement she realized that it helped. Her story included an alcoholic father who once tried to burn the house down when she was a little girl. His erratic behavior confused her and dealing with the love and hatred she felt was difficult. Without going into details I will say that we developed a bond that lasted well after I left the clinic. I heard from her for quite some time and we chatted on the phone. She had married and was pleased to tell me about the kids and their escapades—her marriage and its ups and downs—her jobs—and occasionally we talked through a problem she was having. All this to say that our connection remained strong for a few years after ending therapy. Contact eventually tapered off but I knew we had places in our hearts for each other.

I knew that love fueled our work together. When I say love, what do I mean? It's not easy to explain and others will disagree but for me it means a sort of smiling with my heart. Words that come to mind are nourishing, appreciating, at times awe, commitment, concern, dedication, and hope. Patient's pick up on the therapist's hopefulness so it's important to recognize their positive qualities. Focusing on the negative is something I've never found helpful. Of course problems are discussed and acting out occurs but being able to hold a positive future in mind is picked up by the patient.

The way I see it, non-transferential love in the consulting room, not often talked about, happens over time. It does not preclude frustration or anger. I once asked a despairing patient who knows a lot about gardening whether transplanting an ailing plant into nurturing soil could change it. Of course, plants are not people but the question gave us pause. I was really asking if new experience could be internalized.

As therapist and patient begin to connect, and as the patient begins to see that judgment is not involved, as he is listened to with benevolent curiosity, something happens. A new person emerges and sometimes memories of loving moments with past objects are retrieved. I don't mean the wild, erotic love that sometimes surfaces in therapy as a defense against intimacy, or the transference love for the therapist as past object—and it is not the love that just satisfies our narcissism. It is a love that comes from respect and caring—*caritas* as Shengold (1989) called it. He said:

> *"Only love can ameliorate, and only being able to develop the capacity for love can make meaningful therapeutic contact possible—in life and in therapy."*

Transference, countertransference, the analytic third (Ogden, 2004), and other such concepts fortify us. Soldiers (and we are like soldiers who join our patients in battling demons and protecting hard won insights) do need fortification. Theory protects us. Different models of mind quell our anxiety and provide some kind of order. What we call resistance (I call it reluctance or roadblocks) blames the patient and so eases the pain of rejection therapist's may often feel. I repeat: I think what sustains the dyad during the journey is love or *caritas.*

A special kind of love has made it possible to manage over all these years to maintain my equilibrium while engaging with people whose trust had been shattered. My experience at GHCC was invaluable. It was far from easy but I learned more from my patients than from any book, class, or teacher. These people taught me how to reach them and that being genuine mattered most. To tell the honest truth, I think that when I'm working I'm in some kind of 'other' state—perhaps it is something like a reverie as Ogden calls it or perhaps it's a self-state that Bromberg speaks of. Feeling pushed away and rejected, hated, ignored and also being needed and loved, sometimes all in one session, can play havoc with the emotions. I can't think of another kind of work that keeps one on such a roller coaster. And the sea of words from each patient sometimes threatens to drown us. I recently looked at some process notes from long ago and switching metaphors I saw the density of the jungle we trudge through. That density also sustains us and even when we get lost in it—we keep on going. We know that the end will entail mourning and we wonder how much mourning we can do in our lives? Actually, I wonder if therapists aren't in a sort of perpetual state of mourning with our patients who, as they recover and grow, must mourn their former selves.

I was very fortunate to have found Ella Sharpe in her "Collected Papers" early in my career. Her gift was this:

> *"The urgency to reform, correct, or make different motivates the task of a reformer or educator, the urgency to cure motivates the physician, but the deep seated interest in people's lives and thoughts must be transformed in the clinician, into an insatiable curiosity, free to range over every field of human experience and activity, free to recognize every unconscious impulse, with only one urgency, namely, a desire to know more, and still more. When we react to something that causes us to think 'I cannot understand how a person can think or behave like that' curiosity has ceased to be benevolent."*

There are few answers in our work so filled with questions.

But, you may say, "how can that be possible? Are we not doing this to help people ease their misery? Lessen their anxiety?" Yes, that is our hope but we must temper it with humility. Creating a space for our patients, where they can begin to feel safe enough to speak—to put their miseries and joys into words—is our only real function. Because using words to express oneself is curative in itself. Analysts provide that space in different ways and the analytic frame supports us. All of us are explorers—seeking to understand what so often seems unfathomable. Our knowledge of development helps us try to explain—but each day we learn something that makes us question our cherished beliefs. Only recently have we been freed from the idea of stages and phases. Rona Knight, the Boston Change Process group, and many others have challenged the idea of set stages. Also, each theory we learn gives us a different perspective. We are more artists than scientists although our research is becoming increasingly more sophisticated thanks to neuroscientists and infant observers. Theories are like an artist's palette filled with both old and new pigments, or like a pantry filled with condiments and staples we use when cooking. As we listen to patients we need sustenance. However, one problem is that old theories can be limiting. Perhaps they should have an expiration date. Rona Knight's research (2021) refutes some of the ideas posed by Melanie Klein, Freud, and even Winnicott all of whom had limited instruments of proof and so relied on their own suppositions and imaginations.

Our drive to make sense of things is inborn says Ed Tronick, an eminent development psychologist/researcher. I highly recommend his videos on you tube. He says that we are born with an instinct or drive to *make meaning*. And I believe that this capacity is nurtured by our own experiences of love and disappointment. Our early feelings of omnipotence are never fully relinquished and the unrequited love we have all experienced is never really forgotten. Are these the basis for our wishes to understand? As analysts we learn to tame our judgmental streaks in the service of the 'need to make meaning.'

For me, the love part is a state of mind that I go to in order to work and to write. Many frown on my use of the word love and feel it should be reserved for intimate relationships. But if what we do is not intimate, we are in trouble.

I know no other word to describe what I feel. Love is made up of respect, enthusiasm, passion, platonic and erotic feelings, curiosity, caring, compassion, and deep appreciation that offsets the disillusionment that can lie in wait.

I end up asking those of you who are reading this to join me in wondering how can we summon the state of love? We all have different ways. Do we surround ourselves with family, friends, and animals, art? Do we feed our selves well enough? Music is important to me and I listen a lot. Being creative requires a kind of love. And laughter—so freeing! These are all food for the soul.

Benevolent curiosity is a huge part of being in love. When you are in love, the subject is held in high esteem, faults are disregarded, and criticism melts away. You want to know everything about the person or thing you love. I remember the long phone conversations with my husband to-be and although I can't remember what on earth we talked about it was the connection that mattered.

Things can be loved too. Some people fall in love with a profession, a sport, paintings, music, a hobby—to which they dedicate themselves heart and soul. This 'state of loving' diminishes the normal hatred, envy, impatience, and rage we all harbor. The love that we feel for our work enables genuine attention without judgement. This helps when we experience a patient's rage—whether it is deserved, projected, or a remnant of split off and reawakened feelings. When a patient is telling me off and attacking me a part of me may feel injured or angry, but most of me remembers who I am and my curiosity takes hold. I also appreciate the trust involved when a patient expresses feelings.

Analysts usually don't admit to expressing their own anger but we are human and we do human things. I remember raising my voice in exasperation at my first analytic patient who had been complaining and raging at me for weeks. I was in supervision at the time and dreaded telling my supervisor that one day I angrily said: *"Stop! I have listened to these complaints and insults for long enough. Now is the time to figure out what they mean—to figure out who, why, and what you're really talking about."* The supervisor, to my surprise, said it was about time! My raised voice worked and perhaps I should have stopped the patient sooner—but what we call abreaction (letting loose) can lead to insight. This particular patient responded by sitting up and looking at me. As she did something clicked. She saw me and realized that I was a stand in for someone else. That was the beginning of her remembering a very chaotic childhood. Her abreaction was helpful to a point—she had needed to berate me but after a while she needed a jolt and I responded. I did not plan to raise my voice—I just did. We were both surprised and relieved.

Some of the things I love in no particular order are:

My husband, who was always inspiring and is always there even now that he is gone.

My daughter who battled a life threatening illness with courage and dignity and who I consider a remarkable woman and dearest friend.

My dog Dobbie who came into my life when I was five and never left my side for thirteen years.

Django, JJ, and Jamie—dogs found over the years, wandering the streets—one flea ridden, another practically hairless and so skinny—each blossoming into fluffy, beautiful, sweet and independent companions.

Trees—in the woods and in Washington Square Park—old, sturdy, graceful.

Elephants, loyal, caring of each other, heroic, and sadly, endangered.

Music, a place I can retreat to and feel safe in.

Jazz musicians who go to the edges to create something new.

Memories of my home town—a refuge from a scary house.

Horses—the beautiful creatures on whose backs I gained confidence and mastery. I remember their names to this day.

Two years spent in Carson City.

Pansies whose faces cheered me as a lonely little girl.

My parents.

Perhaps you who read this will make your own list.
I still believe that loving and being loved makes all the difference.

CHAPTER 2

A MEANDERING JOURNEY

"The real voyage of discovery consists,
not in seeking new landscapes,
but in having new eyes."
— *Marcel Proust*

A journey is a person in itself; no two are alike.
And all plans, safeguards, policing, and coercion are fruitless.
We find that after years of struggle that we do not take a trip; a trip takes us.
— *John Steinbeck*

Psychoanalytic work is like a meandering journey inward, and one remarkable feature of it is that you can leap from place to place (as I do in this chapter) in a nano second. Visits to each port of call with an experienced and reliable companion sheds light on what has inhibited continued development[2]. As the dyad travels it gains the strength necessary to arrive at the destination: freedom.

2 How human beings grow, change, adapt, and mature across various life stages.

No passports or tickets are necessary. Imagined past, documented past (diaries, photos, reminiscences, home movies,) the present moment, the wished for or dreaded future, and all the places in between are visited, revisited, re-experienced, reviewed, as often as one wishes. Vehicles of travel are words, actions, silences, and expressed emotions like shame, pride, rage, longing, love, and guilt that take the travelers to places heretofore unexplored. As vision deepens, the sights take on new depth and color.

Along the way the travelers develop a relationship that grows stronger—a relationship that can survive all kinds of weather. As with any travel, this journey requires time and money. A good travel agent can be found at state accredited psychoanalytic institutes through their referrals services, through trusted friends, or *Psychology Today.* A range of travel expenses are available.

People embark on the journey for various reasons such as inhibitions, depression, anxiety, psychosomatic symptoms or illnesses, difficulty in relationships, addictions, feeling lost or stuck—all of which cause psychic pain and sometimes psychic numbness. How they embark varies and is often an indication of the severity of their problems.

As the dyad travels they will experience playful times and also strong undertows, storms, even earthquakes. What then? This is a good question and it brings to mind Freud's analogy of the horse and rider with the horse as the id or unconscious, and the ego as the rider who tames it. In my travel analogy the rider or traveler along with the guide/companion/therapist work together to strengthen the rider so that the storms (horse/storms/unconscious) become less formidable and more tolerable. These storms belong to the patient and they have different meanings. One purpose is to illustrate the intensity of feelings; one may be an expression of anxiety and rage; another may alert the guide to fragility; and another can be a test of the guide's capabilities.

My own first journey at age eighteen had a rocky start. Although I eventually learned a lot, I was not prepared. The most important lesson I learned was about embarking. First the patient and analyst need to click which is usually based on an unconscious vibe. Then the patient hopefully takes responsibility for asking certain questions. In my case, due to my age and naiveté, I think the doctor might have educated me a bit. And even had I been older and more sophisticated, I still think the way to begin analysis is with a degree of explanation about the process offered by the analyst. Blank screen type analysts are passé.

I knew nothing about psychoanalysis and for some reason my analyst seemed not to take that into account. This was way before Tony Soprano and Dr. Melfi, or Billy Crystal and Robert De Niro in *Analyze This*. Pointing to the couch and instructing me to say whatever came to mind sounded bizarre to me. Now, as I look back to the 1950s I see how much things have changed. Had this well-meaning psychiatrist taken the time to explain something about the treatment I believe I would have experienced a better beginning. Beginnings require reasonable preparation. After listening to the prospective traveler, I explain how I work and invite the patient's questions about what I propose during the consultation phase which may consist of one to three sessions. While I talk the prospective traveler has time to assess my confidence, my style, and whether I will be critical or respectful.

When I began to see patients, I learned over time how each one defended herself against the storms that threatened to overpower her. Stepping aside is a popular method of defense that takes the form of dissociating or mentally leaving the scene. I believe that there are many forms of and degrees of dissociation. Not everyone floats up to the ceiling though this is often how dissociation is described. There are different forms of leaving the scene, some momentary, others more permanent and those that lie in between. Day dreaming—something we all do—is a way to avoid a painful moment or an ongoing situation. Another way is denying a danger by actually not feeling it. As we mature we find other ways to protect ourselves but if these methods that we call defenses are overused they end up depriving us of the joy life offers. One common defense is projection whereby we assign our own feelings to others. Owning these feelings becomes possible during the journey. The anxieties of childhood were meant to warn us of danger—but danger is relative, and what felt dangerous as a child does not usually apply to the adult. Why? Because the adult has more sophisticated language and other skills not available to the young child. Even size plays a role in gaining new perspective. As anxieties that once made paying attention difficult diminish, the ability to learn increases. Most travelers, however, still use the early defenses because the past haunts them. While traveling these fears diminish as new vistas provide new views.

With the cessation of symptoms and the removal of roadblocks new choices become available for the patient who continues to grow during the journey. The travel itself strengthens muscles necessary for resilience. Both parties on the voyage learn together how to approach the many bumps along the journey of life by developing better shock absorbers.

I see psychoanalytic work as a collaborative process with two people working towards solving problems. The bond they create grows as they travel and is healing in and of itself. In the nineteen fifties and sixties and sometimes even today, the doctor patient tilt dominates the picture. I believe that when an adult seeks help, the therapist's respect sets a positive tone. Although the psychoanalytic process centers on discovering how the past influences the present by exploring perceptions based on transference distortions observed in treatment, it is the new relationship that makes this possible. The tilted relationship resembles a parental one and may fail for that reason.

I am suggesting a developmental understanding of this work. By reconstructing the earliest thrusts towards separation and individuation that create one's foundation, the dyad creates a new opportunity to set this developmental process back on track. Transferences and other clues can point us to where a person's development was thwarted. The connection formed by the analytic dyad can and does address and affect what lays beneath transference: perception. An un-individuated child with a history of abuse will perceive the world far differently than will a child from a loving home. Developmental tasks such as differentiating self and object, separation and individuation that are basic to how we perceive others will be affected. What I am suggesting is that if we connect with the patient and face what transpired in the past together, it will be the patient who over time will correct the distortions that plague her.

I understand that allying ourselves with the patient can be difficult because of the unconscious representational world and the buried fantasies that affect us all so powerfully, but I have seen that being a real, non-judgmental listener/guide/companion can have a powerful effect too. New sights can make old ones less prominent. In fact it is the analyst as new object that gradually and eventually will be internalized. This is why I propose leveling the playing field in order to establish this important collaboration.

As I have traveled with unique individuals, I have learned that many of the rules I learned early in my career do not hold up, especially the blank screen analyst. Sharing certain life experience when appropriate can offer an example of negotiating life that may interest a patient. *Oh, but that's not analysis* many will say. I must ask if our allegiance is to a theory that restricts us to interpretation or clarification or is our allegiance to our patient's growth? Traveling includes conversation beyond interpretation and free association. There are times when we offer our experience in a situation the patient is faced with by saying something like: *"I remember a time when I felt what you're describing and I tried xyz."* It shows the patient that there are many ways to face situations without giving advice. Becoming selective is a newly acquired benefit of being an adult.

An extension of Freud's thinking is the theory of internal self and object representations that can be regarded as being in large part determined by the young child's phantasy life, by the images it has of objects in its phantasy life, and of the way these phantasy objects relate to and are related to by the child (Joffe and Sandler, 1968). It is thought that pictures of the self and other made of multi-dimensional images or wispy fragments of experience are registered by the brain early in life, sometimes making it difficult to see beyond them for they serve as templates for future relationships. These pictures and feelings we experience with early caretakers are filtered by our age-appropriate needs such as hunger and the need to be held, creating impressions that make up what we call the representational world. Many analysts believe that the representational world basically determines how we experience life and wonder if these representations ever change. I think they can be clothed differently as several things happen. First, and perhaps most important is a new awareness. Vision becomes more acute as we gain new perspective. Early defenses like projection hopefully fade away as the self strengthens. What was once so frightening becomes less so as words replace powerful fantasies.

Loewald (1960) presented us with the idea of the 'analyst as new object' and there is no question in my mind that new experiences with new objects can override the original ones. We are born with genetic propensities but these are shaped by our interaction with others and the culture we share. These interactions influence our perception and vice versa. We tend to use early experiences to guide us. If a parent was perceived as harmful or dangerous (due to reality combined with the child's own aggressive wishes) the child transfers his fear or hatred on to other authority figures, worrying that the danger will be repeated and hoping it won't. This is reasonable and although it takes a long voyage I have seen impressive modifications in this fantasy.

Sam married a very controlling woman who was just like his mother. He unconsciously thought that he could change her thereby mastering his early trauma. But he also wished to preserve the familiar because if felt safe. After a long analysis during which he experienced the analyst as safe enough, Sam gradually let go of his wish to change his mother representation as he continued separating and individuating. I discuss this in more detail in the chapter on masochism.

I believe that the analytic travel companion must prove that he is trustworthy in all types of weather and in all terrains so that he is experienced as insuring safety. Patients often test the co-traveler to make sure he is reliable as Lois did in Chapter Three.

Of course, positive experiences are registered and influence us as well. But the bottom line is that we could not manage without parent figures in childhood and whether they were kind or malevolent, we never forget this reality. This may contribute to masochism where even painful connection is better than no connection. It is as though the child says "I'll do anything if you care for me." And sometimes the tables are turned when the child sees that his parents bow to its tantrums by behaving masochistically. This is another reason we see powerful resistance in analysis. Feeling safe is a priority and in striving to be independent, it is necessary to feel capable of insuring one's own safety. Early experiences are usually mixed so they have dual effects of resisting and strengthening the collaborative connection in therapy. If a patient makes and keeps the first appointment, I register that as strength enough to proceed. It takes strength and hope to seek assistance and I am always surprised that people consider it as a weakness. It takes courage to travel.

The process of developing, of growing up, is more complex than we can ever really know. Each multi-layered experience is registered by the brain and we are just beginning to understand how this affects us. What happens depends not only on the outside object or event, it also depends on our inborn needs and abilities to perceive and react at specific times. It includes hormones that affect the brain. Experience is multi-directional. I don't think we can ever fully appreciate the complexity of how and what a child notices and registers. Instead both Freud and Klein "adultomorphized" the young child by postulating what they think and feel. Whole theories are built on these imposed fantasies that can never be proven scientifically. Babies give us enough clues about their comfort and mood without our having to impose our own fantasies on them.

In fact, Freud's use of the oedipus in plays by Sophocles and Shakespeare's Hamlet as the centerpiece of psychoanalysis has become a shibboleth that has no scientific evidence to lend it credence. Instead Freud used circumstantial evidence, specifically his own dreams and self analysis to support his theory. John Ross (1982) in his paper on Laius, traces the history of Oedipus and presents important ideas on Freud's use of the story. Freud's use of these dramas reflected his own dilemmas perhaps featuring the incest wishes to entice his audience. Best sellers usually include sex, murder, intrigue, and betrayal. Did Oedipus with its themes of parricide explain Freud's own inner conflicts that are shared by many men with similar backgrounds? Is this one of those things that if we look for it we find it? Psychoanalysis sees everything in terms of poor Oedipus and only a few have openly challenged his centrality. Freud must have been aware of Oedipus' childhood trauma perpetrated by Laius (a pederast) and his mother Jocasta and chose as his focus the incest theme, ignoring Oedipus' early trauma perpetrated by these paranoid parents. We can all agree that a child's wish to be an adult is normal, and this includes rebellion and rejection of parental ideas; and we see that some children speak of marrying mommy or daddy—part of pretending to be like adults. Some children want one parent to disappear because two is company and three is a crowd. But, framing these wishes in sexual terms skews the picture. Yes, children have sexual feelings and fantasies but do they really want to fornicate with a parent, or do they want unconditional love and affection? I look at the Oedipus Complex as a metaphor describing the conflict between wishes to grow up and wishes to remain a child. Childhood, depending on the circumstances, is a time of joy and pain. But all children experience painful feelings of exclusion. And so of course, pretending to be adults is common. It is a necessary rehearsal. It also assuages the pain of exclusion. Wishes to marry mommy or daddy could represent the wish for exclusive attention. We can even speak of killing the parents—the older generation as Loewald (1979) did but could this also be a defense against the reality of losing them? Or could this wish to kill 'the father or mother' be retaliation for their letting them go, in Oedipus' case, abandonment? After all, they did leave this baby after tying his feet together to die. And as much as children want to be adults they also wish to be cared for and protected. Is castration anxiety an unconscious wish to remain a child? Or is it a projection? And finally, was Freud's separation anxiety too shameful for him to admit? There is the conundrum: leaving childhood or becoming a responsible adult?

I think Oedipus represents the difficulties of growing up with all its challenges, many of which were caused by the older generation represented by Laius who, faced with his own mortality, and his own traumatic childhood, took revenge on his child. Is not this the intergenerational transmission of trauma writ large? Had Laius not been so damaged, had he lived a good life, would it have mattered? And how did Freud manage with his young narcissistic mom who kept having children and who expected so much from him—her golden Sigie? Breger (2009) tells an interesting story and I encourage reading his book.

Research based on observation of children, according to Rona Knight (2011), tells us that development is fluid and goes on throughout life, not just at specific stages as Freud and others believed. Margaret Mahler and Daniel Stern, both baby researchers, have enriched our theories as have Beatrice Beebe and Frank Lachmann with their important, scientific research. Preceding them John Bowlby's work (1940 and 1960) deserves our gratitude. He emphasized the actual history of the relationship between mother and baby. He believed that children responded to real life events and not primarily to unconscious fantasies as Melanie Klein had proposed. Bowlby was influenced by Winnicott and they both agreed that humans come into the world with predispositions that are sensitive to the social interactions necessary to healthy development. But while Bowlby was interested in how a child's environment is internalized and affects the child's development, Winnicott was more interested in the way the inner world engages with and is affected by external events. Bowlby and Mary Ainsworth (1978) did amazing work by observing children—work that inspired Mary Main (2000), Peter Fonagy (2003), and Jon Mills who in his book *Treating Attachment Pathology (2005)* discusses clinical issues. Mills sees attachment pathology as a disorder of the self causing interpersonal discord that fuels and sustains myriad forms of clinical symptomatology. Allan Schore (2009), a leading authority on how our right hemisphere regulates emotion and processes our sense of self offers evidence that emotional interactions reflect right-brain-to-right-brain affective communication. According to Schore, the brain is structurally organized to regulate affects when patient and therapist develop a healthy connection based on empathic communication.

You may ask what these ideas have to do with the journey. As I mention in Chapter Five, what we view as oedipal guilt needs reviewing as does the meaning of castration anxiety. When we visit the isle of masochism and what causes it, the open mind will help.

The infant needs food and positive connection. The toddler, needs support with degrees of freedom, the adolescent needs self-esteem to engage with the world. The mental representations of selves and others form the background we draw on to move along through life. A major goal of the psychoanalytic journey is to examine these representations and templates and to either work towards adjusting them or replacing them with new experiences. My major question is: does the reliving through a transference neurosis serve to ingrain negative experiences in the brain or does the collaboration with the analyst as co-traveler provide a new experience that allows one to switch to new neural pathways.

The good enough guide/companion on the journey will do her best to follow her partner, adding her perceptions when applicable because she is also an actual subject, not just an object that is a product of transferences. The analyst's ability to relate on an even playing field illustrates her respect. I think that instead of looking down and offering what we call interpretations, we analysts should offer our thoughts and observations at appropriate times leaving ample room for our patient's opinion. Conversation is strengthening. Regarding free association: in my mind, conversation is a form of free association between two people. During these conversations the co-traveler can say something like: *tell us more about xyz—what comes to your mind?* This is what we analysts normally do and the question becomes part of the patient's modus operandi. Introducing the idea of seeing what comes to mind is really quite pleasurable.

As the dyad travels they may visit pioneers like Loewald, Ferenczi, Sandler, Freud, along with more recent theorists like Mitchell, Ogden, Tronick and many others. Just imagine being invited to dinner by any one of them—or even all of them. By the way, we are taught not to suggest readings to our patients but why not? Both travelers can feel free to recommend (not assign) movies, books, articles—all in the service of exploring and connecting. I realize that this is an interactive model I propose and many analysts will say "that's not analysis." But why not? Intellectualization has been seen as a defense but is it not also an ego strength? I favor combining the intellectual understanding with the emotional—blending them. Also, Freud (1914) said:

> "*Any line of treatment or investigation which recognizes the fact of unconscious, or transference or resistance, takes them*

> *as the starting point of its work and regardless of its results, is psychoanalysis."*

Recognizing each other as unique individuals with a common purpose is a often new experience and one that presents new ideas for consideration. As the analytic journey proceeds a bond develops—a bond of respect and as Shengold called it 'caritas' which means love. Not the erotic or romantic love, although they are often experienced, but the compassionate love that entails deep respect and concern. Both are said to produce the hormone oxytocin—the love hormone.

Can we change the early templates or neuronal pathways? Maybe not, but we can uncover here-to-fore unused pathways, or even form new ones. I think of trail blazing—gaining the courage to leave the well-worn path. Again I mention Doidge's (2007) excellent example in the first chapter of *The Brain That Changes Itself.* In this chapter he tells us about a man who lived a long and active life following a miraculous recovery from a major stroke that had left him completely immobilized and unable to speak. His autopsy showed that the brain had either created new neuronal pathways along side the damaged area or most likely had unmasked previously existing, possibly dormant pathways which accounted for the neuroplastic rewiring. The original damage was still visible. The loving and steady care given this victim by his psychiatrist son brought him back to full functioning by starting from scratch—crawling like a baby. His other son was Paul Bach-y-Rita, a famous neuroscientist who went on to introduce sensory substitution as a tool to treat patients with neurological disorders.

As Loewald (1960) suggested, the analyst has the opportunity to utilize the power conferred by the analysand to become a new object. Functioning as a guide/partner the analyst may be perceived simultaneously and alternately as an omniscient, omnipotent being whom the analysand desperately needs, and as a de-idealized equal who can be questioned, doubted, criticized, competed with, defeated, loved, and ultimately given up when no longer needed. However, I don't agree that the analyst is totally 'given up'—I think her functions are internalized. The analyst needs to be able to recognize when it is important to accept, go along with, and explain the use that the analysand is making of her at any particular time.

Another way to look at this is by seeing that as analyst and analysand connect over time they co-create a new relationship often referred to as *the third* (Ogden, 1994), vastly different from the patient's earliest relationships. This new connection competes with the earlier painful ways of relating. The analyst is at first perceived through the lenses, desires, and anxieties formed earlier in life combined with what the analyst displays about herself. The décor of the office factors in along with the way she dresses, speaks, and looks in general. It is amazing how many things people register when they meet someone new and much of it is unconscious. Same goes for the analyst. So right away the dyad sends messages to each other both overtly and subliminally. The analyst's travel background prepares her to notice things, and some things may register unconsciously. How we react to each person we meet is extremely complex and often out of our awareness. We call this transference, and it happens all the time to everyone. One analyst (Bird, 1972) called transference an ego function. After all, we do rely on experience. Think of the last party or gathering you attended. Someone caught your attention. Why? Looks, posture, dress, accent, height, smile, frown and so on. Each of us is primed to notice what has meaning for us. We are sometimes unaware of odors, timbre of the voice, and something we call vibes, but they count. All this to say that we notice more than we know. Also, people are skilled at finding anything that will satisfy their wishes, wishes that are not necessarily conscious. We all tend to look for the familiar which is one reason we choose friends and partners who will replicate the past. What is familiar feels safe even when painful. The analyst, as partner, refuses to play the part sometimes assigned. A patient may expect criticism or judgment, things he has experienced before, and will try to provoke the analyst. Often people project their own feelings on to another. During his first meeting with an analyst Tom heard the analyst through ears that actually distorted the analyst's voice. As much as he wanted relief from his misery, he feared letting go of what was familiar. He was determined to find reasons not to begin therapy. Alice had the opposite reaction. She was in need of acceptance and so she found it. All this happened instantly and subliminally. We are all good at finding what we look for.

All of us have experienced the calamities of growing up—but when parent figures are unavailable or abusive these rough times become traumatic. Freud (1914) in *Remembering, Repeating, and Working Through* told us that unless we put our thoughts into words and subject them to the light of day we will keep repeating them in actions. This is basically the idea of psychoanalytic work whether done once or five times a week, using a chair or couch. Two people speak, dream, and react to each other by remembering, often through repeating the past in the present. It stands to reason that frequent meetings help.

Today we realize that reviewing and adjusting our beliefs is a long process. Changing our lenses improves vision. The connection between analysand and analyst—both positive and negative—is the fuel. Without such meetings, people do the same thing in every day life, usually choosing someone who will dance the familiar dance. The mailman, the teacher, the spouse, the child—are all perceived in the shadow of and as reflections of the past. We naturally transfer our past perceptions and the feelings they engender into our present lives. A life can be fulfilling by acting on past experience. But all too often, a person becomes crippled by past abuses. Such habits as avoidance of intimacy, procrastination, denial, phobic behavior, pessimism and the depression these habits foster, increase in intensity as we grow older thus depriving us of success and joy.

Because the template of abuse, whether it be physical, emotional, caused by early illness, loss, abandonment, over stimulation, or neglect, affects how one navigates life in general, it takes years of exploration, understanding, and most importantly the experience of a special, new travel companion to recover. The traveling partnership can modify the effects of early on-going stresses with consistency, empathy, optimism/enthusiasm, and reliability. The plasticity of the brain suggests that as a result of long term, intensive psychoanalytic work new patterns and perceptions can occur. Learning a new language—the language of the unconscious or the split off self-states that Bromberg speaks of, affects the brain. The love/caritas experienced in the dyad, sometimes erotic, sometimes platonic, produces oxytocin which affects how we see the world.

It takes two to transform ghosts into ancestors—and this is why a therapist who has training in ghost busting is valuable.

One of the outcomes of psychoanalytic work may be forgiveness as one lays to rest the ghosts that once haunted us. As treatment progresses, the analysand gradually puts into words the envy fueled rage she has split off or acted out and invested in past and present self and object representations which often show up in our self-states. The lenses through which we see have been shaped by early impressions of perceived reality which include the fantasies formed early in life. In many instances parent figures have actually been abusive, neglectful, and pathologically narcissistic. The manner in which all these early figures and their actions are internalized includes the child's needs, perception, and their own age-appropriate ability to process relationships and events. A two-year-old is not expected to experience a parent's neglect or even disappearance the same way as a six year old does. By working in and out of the transference, such experiences take on new shape and the inner object world either changes or is replaced. Perceptions that had been black and white and one dimensional become shaded with color and depth. Self esteem builds as the ego strengthens and the superego loses its harshness. Another way to think of this is that new self-states join and even replace old ones on the stage of life depending on the situation. A six-year-old may be exposed to a teacher who presents new experiences that lead to self-esteem. In high school what we learn depends a lot on our feelings about the teacher. And it stands to reason that travel companions learn new things from and with each other. The analyst's job is sweeping away the detritus that impedes one from moving ahead. As this goes on the lenses widen and vision deepens. Reparations are made and the energy once spent on suppression, denial, projection, isolation of affect, and other character defenses is freed. Mending of splits, along with the internalization of the analyst as new object permit the loving aspects of the self to take center stage. Empathy grows. Anger is expressed, diminishes, and subsides. Forgiveness is possible. This rosy picture often takes a very long time to paint for certain patients. But the very act of painting is growth promoting.

The opposite of the psychoanalytic journey would be staying home, recreating the perceived world day after day and minute after minute, strengthening the early brain pathways. Breathing in the stale air of the past leads to lethargy, depression, and disease. Cults, religions, and other institutions are based on unhealthy needs that crowd out individuality. They recreate the original family with all its good but mostly bad aspects. Authority, bullying, deceit and secrecy erase the potential of collegiality, cooperation, and generativity.

Emma

Emma came to therapy after her third break-up knowing they had all been her fault. "I just don't know what to do when someone loves me" she explained in her first session. "I chase a man and then when I catch him I push him away. What is wrong with me" she wanted to know.

Emma came five minutes late to her fifth session of the week. Breathless and sweaty (heat wave) she collapsed onto the couch and sighed:

> *Pt: I rushed—but left late and the subway was slow. A man next to me was talking to himself—creepy. Work was crazy—Ann* (boss) *was leaving for a conference and getting her stuff together—Jesus. She is so disorganized. I should be boss—why aren't I? What keeps me back?* (getting agitated) *We go over and over this stuckness of mine and it leads nowhere. Sure, I lack ambition and just watch the world go by. My friends are all moving ahead, but not me... not poor Emma. Poor Emma—such a familiar saying. Mom always called me that when I felt left out. But it was with such annoyance. Why was I poor Emma? I was pretty, smart, but so god-damned shy. Look you in the eye? Not easy, and she told me I had to. She was always telling me what to do, how to do it, why, when and if I didn't, she'd keep at it. She never wanted me in the first place and she made that clear when she was drunk.* (silence) *You seem very organized. Neat office, and always on time.*

Emma's observation got me thinking that I am not one of those super-organized folks and since this was our second year of work together, five times a week, I wondered why Emma hadn't picked up on that. The books and papers on my desk were hardly ever neatly stacked. Was she 'transferring' a picture she had of her mom on to me?

After a while, I asked her:

Th: "Do you think you see me like you saw your mom—and if so, where does that take you?"

Pt: *yessss, we've been over this before. I can't seem to help it 'cause I know so little about you. Even after two years I wonder what you're really like. I know you don't judge me like she did, but I keep feeling you really do. Maybe I want to see you like my mom—to keep you away—sort of on the other side, like I keep her. Oh, I had a dream with you and me getting drunk together. We went dancing and things got sexy. I came on to you and you didn't pull away. Does that mean I'm gay?"*

Instead of turning the question back to Emma I decided to answer and said:

Th: "I think it means you want to feel intimate — close — sort of letting your hair down with me. Not worrying about how well you or I are organized." Suddenly, Emma began to cry. Deep sobs that lasted for some minutes. As the tears subsided, she said with wonderment: "I never realized how I long for her love, her arms around me, her acceptance."

This trip to the isle of longing taught us both about her past, her wishes for the present, and how the lack of acceptance early on and throughout her life was affecting her chances for building real self-esteem that would lead to a fulfilling future. Emma had faced some of her pain, and it lightened as she shed the heavy equipment that had been making progress difficult. She realized that by choosing men who were critical and unavailable, she was repeating her relationship with mother. Now she had me and as she allowed me in to offset her mom's messages, we hoped she would change her object choices. I had reworked my own disappointment with my own mother, as Emma had to do. I knew how hard that was. Every child wants and needs a mother's love and that need is hard to let go of. Lives are spent trying to get it. Only when individuation is accomplished can the unique self take center stage. When it does, when separation from mother is achieved, only then can real self-esteem provide the fuel to move on. 'Working through' is a lifetime process, and completing a psychoanalytic journey means that the explorers are equipped to keep exploring on their own.

There are hellish places on the journey. Places you don't really want to visit—but you do. The reason you don't want to visit is the pain. The pain often has to do with punishing yourself for not living up to some unrealistic picture you create, often based on admired others (your ego ideal.) But, that unrealistic picture was formed early in life when what Winnicott called *the false self* is constructed. A false self, he thought, is formed by the child when its mother is unable, for whatever reason, to attune herself to her child. The child squelches its own needs, its spontaneity and self-initiative and instead adapts to the mother's moods as best it can. We all do this to some degree but when there is no spontaneity in life, no chance to play, depression is one result. Mr. M discussed in *Roadblocks on the Journey of Psychotherapy* is a good example (Hall, 2004).

If we don't face and greet this dark side we will continue to trip and fall—to disappoint ourselves in our everyday lives. Sometimes we project our own self-criticism on to others. One patient who never felt loved by her mother was actually unable to hear compliments. It was as if she never could digest this strange new food. Newell Fischer (2019), in his book *Nine Lives,* speaks of malabsorption disease.

But taking the journey with a co-traveler makes it more possible to explore the dark side by shining light on it. If you don't, you will prevent yourself from excelling beyond a certain point. Some people drug themselves with food, drink, heroin, or cocaine. Others develop eating disorders that compromise their health. Psychosomatic illnesses and weakened immune systems can result. It is the purpose of the inner voyage to discover what causes such detours so that new trails are blazed. New vision and new muscles develop along the way and, just like in mountain climbing, you reach plateaus where you rest and enjoy the vistas but you keep climbing to the top. Why? Because you can.

As the journey progresses, the patient tells the stories of her life. She tells them in different ways and, as she travels, she finds old friends and enemies, places she had forgotten about, events that stand out, and emotions and fantasies that were buried or split off. As she gradually puts into words the love and hatred, the envy-fueled rage, the fears of separation, the dread of dependency, and the pain of unrequited love, laughter and a new richness emerge, often in relationships with others but also when alone. Scenes shift. New light casts different shadows that permit new vision. Shame, once buried, diminishes with the light. Guilt is alleviated. Intimacy becomes possible. Needs change. Talents blossom. The pain and struggle are soon forgotten.

I believe that travel always deepens one's perception.

CHAPTER 3

SELF-MURDER

When the life force is stifled, homicide and suicide are born.
— Jane Hall

Put your sorrow into words. The grief you keep inside
you will whisper in your heart until it breaks.
— Shakespeare, *Macbeth*

This chapter is dedicated to Leonard Shengold and to Haydee Faimberg. *Soul Murder* (1989) is a text that has had a profound effect on our understanding of trauma, loss, despair, and psychic repair. Haydee Faimberg (2005) whose seminal work on the intergenerational transmission of trauma has broadened and deepened my understanding of this psychological calamity.

Strain trauma is the concept that describes the impairment of normal psychological development of the child in the absence of sufficient and reliable love, safety, and security. Too often the anxiety, rage, and depression of the primary caretaker(s) are translated into physical, verbal, and/or emotional abuse and neglect that are then directed toward their children. These assaults require the developing child to erect defenses that protect and shield them in whatever ways possible.

The child in these settings, one who is constantly criticized, ignored, abused, cannot develop the self-esteem necessary to move ahead in the world, starting with the critical developmental step of being able to separate from the caretaker. One common way to remain connected while at the same time separating, albeit in a compromised manner, is via identification with the aggressor. Other familiar psychic compromises are denial, dissociation, and the construction of a false self. Indicators of such abuse include eating disorders, sadomasochism, addiction, promiscuity, attention deficit disorders, and depression that can lead to suicide and, in extreme cases, murder. All too often, the child's own body becomes a repository for this rage.

The following case, a composite sketch of several patients, illustrates some common themes reflected in the work with those children described above when presenting as adults in my office.

Lois came to therapy because her husband, John, wanted a divorce and she was devastated. A twenty-one-year-old artist with growing success, she realized that she had not been giving John enough attention. Spending long hours at her studio, lost in her work, made her increasingly unavailable. Lois was very bright and seemed quite able to reflect. She admitted to what she called "a difficult part of her personality," but was unaware of the effect this had on other people, specifically John and eventually me. In fact, she typically *forgot* her many outbursts of rage that were driving her husband away. John's attempts to express love to Lois were quickly forgotten, ignored, or met with withdrawal or even hostility. She did not seem aware of the damage she inflicted and adamantly defended herself when confronted. She completely blocked any memory of her rageful behavior which apparently resided in a split off self-state. Stubbornness was a major thread in her personality. I began to understand it as a lifesaving defense that had once effectively protected her from pain. She experienced her own dependency needs as dangerous and turned them into caring for others. Her fear was realistic given how in her early life her appropriate needs had been ignored. Beginning in childhood, Lois had taken the adult role in her family. She also saw herself as the ugly duckling, without the dazzling wit and glamour that surrounded her. A rather plain looking, slim, petit woman with short, blond hair, blue eyes, and a blue-jean style, Lois was likable, intelligent, engaging and seductive. Over time, I learned about her history, her stubbornness, and how her charm endeared her to others.

Lois, the third child of wealthy, jet-setter, hippie parents was born prematurely while her parents were traveling in India. Three months after her birth her parents left the childcare to servants and a local nanny, as they regularly did, to tour the country. Father had no patience with crying children and her charming mother was "on her own planet." She learned that the older brothers, three and five when Lois was born, teased and taunted their baby sister while a helpless nanny stood by. Lois had no memory of this but during one period of our work, I believe these early years were re-enacted. Lois was being extremely provocative and during a particularly whiny period I had an impulse to shove her away. We talked about this as possibly her way of remembering how it had been with her brothers.

The parents were wealthy and beautiful people. Father, a successful art collector was impatient, volatile, and often physically abusive to mother and brothers, and verbally abusive to Lois. In addition to travelling, the family moved frequently between their several homes.

Mother was a beautiful and seductive woman from a wealthy family. She had been sexually abused by her father, which scarred her deeply and, no doubt, affected her capacity to be a 'good enough' mother. Before the parents' divorce Lois and her brothers were endlessly exposed to the parents' physical and verbal fighting.

Memory: Age eight and left alone for hours (her brothers were at boarding school) in the Paris apartment while her parents went partying. Hours went by before they returned, both drunk. Lois clearly remembered washing the vomit and blood off her mother. Caretaking became a role, that was central in the drama of her childhood. Lois was always the responsible one, there for others, making them laugh, and always needing to feel in control because of the chaos that surrounded her. She believed that her mother sexually abused her eldest brother who she described as handsome and brilliant, and who was eventually accused of abusing one of his children. Brother number one was the handsome genius and brother number two seemed mildly retarded. I wondered if he suffered from an autism spectrum disorder. Lois adored them both. These three siblings formed a unit in the growing family of step sisters and brothers that appeared after the parents' divorce and remarriages.

After the divorce, the children split their time living with their father during the school year then with mother during the summer and other vacation periods. Their mother's second husband was a successful Hollywood producer with adolescent children who lived with him. Movie stars and high-level politicians attended their frequent parties. Father married a famous Broadway actress with whom he had two children. Lois, surrounded by glamour and fame, struggled to fit in. Painting became her refuge and at the age of seventeen she left home to study abroad. She married at age nineteen and came to therapy because after a year of marriage her husband wanted a divorce, complaining that Lois was crazy.

In the first year of therapy during her twice weekly sessions, that increased to three and then four times a week, Lois entertained me with stories about famous people and alarmed me with tales of her turbulent childhood. Beneath her charming facade I quickly became aware of her fragility. One day in the second year of therapy, after a fight with John, she swallowed enough sleeping pills to frighten everyone. After a brief hospitalization she resumed therapy. We discussed increasing her sessions and she agreed.

Lois described her mother as charming and totally self-centered. Memories of her cuddling in bed with her little girl after which she withdrew and ignored her were confusing and naturally upset Lois. Wonderful times spent cooking or shopping together were followed by complete and utter neglect. Drugs and alcohol were part of her parents' lives and Lois never knew what to expect.

Only by paying acute attention to the enactments and my countertransference, was I able to realize just how damaged Lois was. The charm and humor she displayed obscured her desperate attempts to survive. The narcissistic and sporadic affection from her mother was confusing but it was clear that Lois was expected to take care of herself far before she was ready. Boundary setting seemed to fall to Lois, and this is where her stubborn streak proved valuable. "Come close, but only so close" was her message—in life and in therapy. Stubbornness was a weapon that her children seemed to inherit—and, as with Lois, was an expression of anger and also a way to ward off neediness. I came to see that she unconsciously or subtly encouraged her children's' rebelliousness. Faux compliance and charm, mixed with stubbornness, became a way of fighting to maintain the self. This played out in treatment, where periods of feeling connected to me were followed by aggressive and mean-spirited behavior. She felt that her existence depended on being charming and entertaining, and this exhausted her.

Lois seemed to split off her sense of frustration and helplessness; or more specifically, the self-states that contained her neediness and anger were not available to her. This is how she protected herself from feeling an underlying depression. The lack of empathy, that seems characteristic of deprived and traumatized people, is often camouflaged by appearing solicitous. Unable to fully differentiate self and object, the abused adult's caring behavior is, at its heart, selfish in nature. She sees herself in others who become narcissistic extensions. In their day to day living, many narcissistic individuals cannot bear feelings of helplessness and neediness, and instead insist on holding on to the experience of grandiosity. For instance, when confronted with the disappointments and losses of life, they typically have great difficulty in experiencing sadness. Their defenses protect them from painful disappointments.

After several years of treatment Lois and John's relationship had improved and their first child was born. Four more children followed in close order, and Lois reminded me of a Pied Piper. The children adored her singing and dancing and humor, but as they approached adolescence they began to rebel. Separating was difficult for them, and their stubbornness, as if inherited from their mother, helped. Lois was unconsciously passing on her own trauma by clinging to her children while at the same time, appearing to be independent. They began pushing her away in various ways as Lois had been doing to me in treatment on and off from the start. Lois could be stubbornly oppositional with me and then seem like the best, most reasonable patient. I wondered with Lois if her behavior with me was a reflection of how her mother had been both neglectful and endearing with her. We had many conversations about this.

The years of treatment helped Lois curb her volatility and her need to control but she felt that her children and husband provoked her incessantly. Their normal need to rebel was exacerbated by Lois's early needs to control and this became a vicious cycle. By the time she became aware of this, the damage had been done. In the fourteenth year of treatment Lois was grappling with her children's destructive behavior. Her young and adoring angels were becoming devils—that is, very rebellious adolescents. One boy turned to drugs, another got expelled for destroying school property, and one daughter showed signs of an eating disorder. The analysis became a dumping ground for crises. I felt overwhelmed—making referrals for the family took more time than I had.

When they were little, Lois's children had sensed and responded to a fragility in their mother by hugging her and reassuring her of their love. But with the onset of adolescence their rebellion in the service of separating alarmed Lois and John.

Discussion

I have found that such unloved children never *truly* or fully trust another and have subtle yet real ways of fooling the therapist who takes on the role of captive audience. This reflected Lois's childhood where she was bystander to her parent's drama. As Lois gained insight first intellectually and then emotionally, the treatment became precarious because the 'as if' self, or false self, had been exposed and feared death. This is what I describe as Self-Murder. Killing the destructive introject or the false self is homicidal as well as suicidal. Self and object are fused significantly. The concept of self and object differentiation is a complex one that defies clearcut definition. For Lois, and others neglected in childhood, differentiation is fluid at best.

In the beginning of treatment Lois did whatever she could to test my strength and patience, from missing sessions and not calling, refusing to talk for days, threatening to quit, and castigating me. And this was all interwoven with entertaining me while appearing to strengthen our connection. I would be relieved when Lois acted like the "good patient" and in those moments I shared with her that her inconsistency seemed to reflect the dramas of her earliest object relations. Over the years she was able to feel and express her love for me sporadically as her mother had done with her. She became increasingly aware of the split off, repressed anger but the shame of her loss of control with John led to the attempted suicide.

Lois adored me or hated me and it took years before she developed the capacity to hold ambivalent feelings. Interestingly, as this was happening, her paintings became more nuanced, primary colors shifted to more muted tones. This developmental step, the ability to tolerate many feelings about the same person, took the pressure off and served to diminish Lois's need to split. The realization that she could have mixed feelings alleviated much anxiety, yet as she felt closer to me she felt also the threat of losing the equilibrium that had taken so many years to find.

Years were spent building bridges from the past to the present so that letting go of once useful defenses, required before the final phase of analysis, was occurring in our work. I have come to see the resistance to change, which I prefer to call reluctance, as a response to the fear of loss of a sense of herself, as well as of internalized objects. There were times when we could just talk about what was going on—sort of stepping out of the transference. I would say to Lois, who loved reading mysteries: "*Let's figure out what triggers your outbursts with John so that you can feel some control—can we think of it as a mystery to be solved?*"

The whole treatment had been one enactment after another and after years of work it seemed that finally the chickens had come home to roost but not only to settle in and create new life. Rather, Lois began to experience the depression she had warded off for so long, leading to sleeping during the day and leaving her family to fend for themselves. This required that Lois's husband take time off from work. But suddenly the light that had gone out ironically also shone in a way that sometimes shocks those left in the dark. This was effective in bringing the family together such that ongoing family and individual therapy allowed the translation of actions into words.

Experiencing the sadness and anger due to conscious awareness and acceptance of helplessness and neediness, are concomitants of a mourning process which Lois had previously avoided. The analytic working-through provides an opportunity for this mourning to take place; saying goodbye to a grandiose self is painful. Many narcissistic people never do.

Why do I use the term *self-murder* instead of suicide in such cases? Self-murder applies to self-states that reside in the whole self. So self-murder is a literal way of saying that a cohesive self has not been achieved or that self and object differentiation has not occurred. The self-states are at war with one another. Such warfare can be seen as a defense against the unbearable pain of helplessness that was once warded off by the grandiose self-state that must lose its power as development proceeds. Self-murder can also be seen as a beginning differentiation of self and object.

Shengold (1989) spoke of the soul-murder inflicted by physical and emotional child abuse and Haydee Faimberg (2005) wrote about the intergenerational transmission of trauma. Ed Tronick (2011) has written and spoken about epigenetic theory—how genes can be modified or even turned off during stressful times. I don't think we can ever fully know what goes on internally—we can only try.

The murder of a child may start in the womb with lack of prenatal care, or at birth with insecure attachment, and can progress through separation-individuation to adolescence, into parenthood and old age. Neglect may be suffered by rich and poor alike. Beebe and Lachmann (2002) and Stern (1985) tell us that the infant experiences 'being experienced' and so the quality of early attachment (in the first four months) is seen to have profound implications for future development (Bowlby, 1980). Lois and her brothers suffered early loss due to their parent's frequent travel and inability to provide nourishing love, compounded by a frequent change of nannies, in an environment where they were provided for materially but not emotionally. In fact, parenting was toxic.

So many things impinge on what we think of as normal development. Inherited dispositions, ability to extract from the environment, hormones secreted in stress and in love that affect the developing brain, along with diet, epigenetic changes, and things we have not even discovered, all leaving cause and effect still mysterious. What appears as a normal family often hides chilling secrets. But good things happen too, things that therapists may never hear about.

In this chapter I reflected on my experience with patients who were deprived in childhood. They had in common mothers who were ill-equipped to care for and cherish their children as individuals, mothers whose own abusive childhoods and illnesses scarred them. I refer to these mother figures as not good enough, or more precisely, bad enough. This is clearly in contrast to Winnicott's (1953) concept of the good enough mother:

> *"The good-enough mother... starts off with an almost complete adaptation to her infant's needs, and as time proceeds she adapts less and less completely, gradually, according to the infant's growing ability to deal with her failure."*

My definition of the bad enough mother is that she starts off with an inability or disinclination to bond or she may smother her child metaphorically; she may be so distracted that she neglects her baby; she may suffer postpartum depression; physical illness; she does not provide appropriate food at appropriate times; and as time goes by she continues to be unaware of her child's normal developmental needs. Often she has been abused, physically or mentally, leaving her frightened, depressed, and anxious.

How much can analytic work accomplish for the adult children of these bad enough mothers? Are other forms of treatment more suited to the adult whose development was seriously thwarted? While I see each person as unique, and each dyad as special, some commonalities make these questions worth pondering. Can new experience with new objects correct or touch the earliest experience? I was most impressed by Norman Doidge's book on the plasticity of the brain which I have mentioned in other chapters. Perhaps DBT groups that stress mindfulness, emotional regulation, and tolerance of distress help the unique individual. Groups may be effective through identifying with each other. Perhaps with certain patients the transference is overwhelming and regression is too harmful.

Lois and I talked about this and as we did, our connection grew. Yes, it was cognitive or intellectual at first but she was very bright and also a mother who did not want to repeat her own childhood with her children. She refused to try a DBT group. I struggled with how much regression I thought we could and should tolerate. Sometimes we agreed that using the chair was preferable to the couch because looking at each other did serve to hold her together when fragmentation threatened.

After her overdose we sat face to face for a year and then intermittently after that. We had conversations about shame and worked on ways to diminish it through understanding and helping her by strengthening her ego. I encouraged Lois to talk about being an artist and how she felt about her success. It is important to note that it was not through compliments but through her explaining how she worked that allowed her to feel a sense of accomplishment. Outside praise does not work in tackling shame—the fight must go on internally so, as Lois reviewed her work process she shored up prideful feelings. Her paintings were selling well and the income was substantial, her dressing shifted from blue jeans to feminine skirts and colorful tops, she had her ears pierced, and significantly, her husband began complimenting her and their sex life improved.

True individuation, the capacity to acknowledge the difference between self and other, requires accepting one's needs and then mourning their lack of fulfillment. This takes time for adults such as Lois given that early psychological damage and deprivation interferes with the ability to trust others. A great deal of testing goes on that only a prepared therapist can handle, especially since these tests run from the obvious to the subtle. An important but often neglected aspect of the best treatments is that of a clear and reliable frame. And equally important, explanations and conversations work far better than interpretations with such patients in my experience. It is not unusual for severely damaged patients to "defeat" the therapist by leaving and going from one to another; this serial experience of therapy is not unusual and it may be as good as it gets for some patients. When Lois was late paying me early in treatment I said: *Lois, I think I understand how scary it must feel to count on me because of your experience. One way of determining my trustworthiness is by testing me. Hopefully we will find ways to work together but I do need to be paid as we originally agreed.*

One way of looking at what happens when differentiation is not fully accomplished is that the original depriving object, fused with the potential self is kept alive in the internal representational world (Sandler & Rosenblatt, 1962). It is then replicated by finding equally negative relationships that perpetuate the trauma of abuse. Lois had unconsciously provoked John into threatening divorce.

I associate self-murder with preventing growth and in such cases it is easy to understand the sadomasochism so prevalent in life and in therapy. Finding partners who resemble the parent or goading the partner to behave like the original object representations preserves the familiar. I postulate that there are degrees of differentiation that fluctuate in times of stress. In treatment, the extraordinarily painful process of letting go of the bad object is strenuously fought and having a good object available helps to make it possible. It is important to remember that what is familiar, no matter how painful, feels safe; this is one reason the patient tries making the analyst into the original object. The relinquishing of this pathological tie is accomplished, in Freud's (1917) words, *"bit by bit, at great expense of time and cathectic energy, and in the meantime the existence of the lost object is psychically prolonged.*" These words were about the mourning process and I think they apply to Lois.

Lois had an inordinate need and ability to maintain the conscious experience of a grandiose, controlling, self which she imagined was her only avenue of escape. This fantasy of power is taken from the abusive parent by identification and is also a left over from the omnipotent stage of development. It is a defense against helplessness. Both Lois and her mother suffered traumatic helplessness. Constant disappointment wore them down and only their grandiose fantasies sustained them. Lois had traits of the charming psychopath whose parents were not equipped to nurture or provide secure shelter. Her façade, or false self, worked well enough, and she actually became what appeared to the world as a good mother. However, because the children were in large part narcissistic extensions, they had great difficulty leaving home. Delinquent behavior is often a last resort in breaking free; one compromise is jail. I have suggested elsewhere that many prisoners are unconsciously asking to be held and cared for. (See Mr. S. in Chapter One.)

As psychoanalysts, we have seen close-up the effects of what often looks to all the world like normal parenting, but is actually either cold, out of tune, verbally and often physically abusive, neglectful, or extremely controlling. We have seen the effects of this in the children from these families, children who have great difficulty internalizing or even recognizing love as they grow into adulthood. Gestures of love and appreciation from others bounce off those deprived of early and consistent emotional nourishment from their caregivers.

Newell Fischer (2019) in his book *Nine Lives,* calls this malabsorption *disease.* Object constancy is not achieved in such deprived children, thus they never learn to digest loving care and actually seem allergic to it as adults. Hungry for love, security, and praise yet unable to metabolize or even recognize it, the deprived child becomes a desperate adult, never sated. Eating disorders, addictions, fetishes, gambling, promiscuity, and self-cutting are some attempts to deal with the deep loneliness of the love starved, maltreated child. The bond that develops with a good enough therapist over a long period of time can offer new experiences that allow the patient to gradually loosen her ties to the original parent's message: you do not matter. Doidge describes using different neuronal connections in the brain. In this day of chemical solutions, and behavioral therapy, psychoanalytic treatment is the dark horse that will hopefully win the race. And yes, it takes time. Modification is the goal.

In sum, the shame and pain of having a bad enough mother or father results in denial, self-reproach, rage, and avoidance. Victims like Lois are usually labeled as borderline, in the paranoid-schizoid position, on the autistic spectrum, manic-depressive, psychotic, acting out, unable to mentalize, and so on. I suggest letting them out of these boxes and reviewing with these patients over time how the original defenses became character armor that once served a purpose but along the way became crippling. I call this 'explanation' instead of interpretation, offered as a history of childhood stress unfolds in treatment.

The technique I am describing is different from the classical model of blank screen, neutral interpreter of conflict. I present myself as a co-worker using explanation based on respect. Why? I have seen the deprived patient respond more positively when treated as a partner on a level field than they do with an authority who supposedly "has the answers" and who is perceived as looking down on them. I suggest greeting each patient as someone who has done the best they can with the cards they have been dealt. I try to enlist my patients as co-workers in solving problems or mysteries. When transference becomes an impediment to progress I explain what is happening, otherwise we end up repeating the damage. When a patient balks at the invitation to collaborate I may sit back and wait. There is no forcing involved and this seems to help. I suggest facing the problems together—as allies. How is this different from interpreting the transference? I see it as an invitation, a more active intervention—one made in a straightforward manner. Something like: "*Sam, I think we can work together to figure out what caused the problem and then how to approach it. This will take time because it is complicated but I think that together we can figure things out.*" Being candid was not encouraged or suggested when I was a student but I hope that in today's world we can speak freely.

I often start my ideas with "Could it be that...?" or "What occurs to me is.." or "I wonder if this makes any sense...." This inclusion of a patient's opinion is ego building. The contemporary therapist's calm, respectful stance is often the first experience of concern for some patients. I have seen it work over and over. But this is very hard work and not every therapist is cut out for it. And sometimes the work fails. We cannot click with everyone who crosses our thresholds.

If I can interest a patient in taking the journey to explore how the past affects the present we gradually become allies as well as transference figures. Along the way we therapists act as the container by taking in and bearing toxicity; holding it and detoxifying the experiences; returning them in due course in an acceptable form as food for thought, and in this way we construct a new relationship that is meant to compete with the old one. Food for thought is all we can give but it is given with love. It is the gift of a lifetime. I think many of us have made the mistake of trying to boost a patient's self-esteem with praise, enthusiasm, and cheer-leading. It does not work. What does seem to work is validating early experience with empathy. To some degree the therapist's quiet enthusiasm may be felt and appreciated but it is not easily or quickly digested or metabolized. In fact, too much encouragement is like a summer shower on parched land. Our basic work is tilling the soil, preparing it for new growth. Just being there is an underestimated gift. A self-murdering adult stubbornly holds on to her introjects "bad" as they may be, and this stubbornness and these introjects are the therapist's major rivals.

We are seeing people like Tommy in Ann Sexton's poem, Red Roses (Hall, 2004) and Lois to a lesser degree whose ties to the bad object are powerful. There was no mother of rapprochement—no mother to come back to when the world got scary. So the pre-separation-individuation child introjected the mother instead and got stuck, never differentiating enough if at all from this bad object. The very idea of letting her go, as toxic as the bad parent might have been, is unimaginable and we speculate that some self-murders are attempts to murder that bad introject while at the same time holding on forever. The therapist inherits this situation and if she is allowed in it is sometimes with magnetic force. She gets sucked in and is literally cast in the role of bad enough mother. Sometimes it looks as though progress is being made, but this can be deceiving. And as a glimmer of possibility is felt, major regressions often occur. When the original object was psychotically abusive her incorporation makes letting go seem impossible. I think of a suicide bomber with explosives strapped to his chest. The therapist as co-worker and not transference figure helps in such instances. Techniques include mirroring and whenever possible, explaining what's going on. Engaging a patient in conversations is useful so that new ways of perceiving become available. And "being with" as discussed by Purcell (2019). Lois and I talked about movies we had both seen and books we had read and compared our impressions. These conversations built our relationship as we came to respect or even argue with each other's points of view. This is what I mean by a level playing field. "That's not analytic" some will say but why not? Our conversations led to free associating and exploring fantasies and this gave us access to the unconscious.

Both the normal omnipotence of a child and the grandiosity that goes with it cause him to imagine he is responsible for his pain. It is beyond his comprehension that he is helpless. In extreme cases of neglect such as the Romanian Orphans (Greene, 2020) the brain does not develop normally and babies die (Spitz, 1945) or are permanently disabled.

Do we know enough about the guilt that is usually more evident than shame and can actually be used as a defense against it? *"It must have been my fault"* is easier for the child than *"I had nothing to do with it"* because the latter means exclusion and impotence. So guilt can actually be used adaptively. Also, it has been found by neuroscientists that the part of the brain that is associated with empathy does not develop in some traumatized children. It is indeed easier to connect psychopathy to brain anomalies and neuroscientists are finding that extreme stress in childhood causes high levels of cortisol that effect the developing brain. So the jury is out: is psychopathy chemical or psychological. Or is it due to epigenetic changes? Or all three?

I see continued emotional abuse and the sustained or strain trauma it causes, along a continuum. At one end are the various degrees of neglect and at the other is the actual physical and verbal abuse. The latter at least provides connection and sometimes they go together. Most confusing to the young child is the uneven or unpredictable parent who engenders hyper-vigilance. A sunny day can be followed by a stormy one, a hug by a slap. This cycle is repeated in life and in therapy, and often the analyst is seduced into enactment. For instance, after a stormy session we are relieved when the patient can be reflective. Sounds reasonable enough, but are we missing the full meaning of the shift? Are we in fact cast into the child's role of feeling relief after a storm? Or food after hunger? Mood swings may be emblematic of uneven care taking yet we prefer to call them manic-depressive or bi-polar disorders. Sharing such an observation with a patient opens the door to exploration. *"Yesterday you were furious with me and today we can reflect on it. I wonder if this is what it was like when your mom was so unpredictable."* I use the word 'wonder' frequently because it introduces the idea to the patient and because that is what we do. Rarely do we know with certainty. I worry that the certainty that some authors convey can be dangerous because it leads us to making the mysterious into fact. Memories change as development proceeds because perception changes. The way a two year old experiences life is far different that the way a twelve-year-old does. And the degree of differentiation achieved surely affects perception.

We must appeal to the highest level of development in order to think about repairing what has been broken. Even bad enough moms may sometimes be good and the child's anger/relief cycle is repeated throughout life by finding partners who will do the dance, often to sadomasochistic music. But what is repeated depends on perception. For instance when a parent goes away, the infant responds far differently than a teen-ager does. Explanation appeals to the intellectual, problem-solving part of the patient and I have seen it pave the way for emotional understanding. I never dissuade a patient from reading about psychology as some analysts do.

As I write this, I am reminded of a Sunday *New York Times* front-page story about twelve-year-old Maya. She suffered brutal abuse by her stepmother, and was overlooked for years by the City's child welfare system, until one day she was found by a neighbor in a pool of blood and rushed to the hospital where she later died. A social worker assigned to this case had believed Maya's explanations of her bruises and cuts as accidents. No one wants to believe that horrendous abuse really does occur. But Grimm's fairy tales can come true. I wonder if the Grimm brothers were chroniclers of their times. Childhood fears are all to often based on reality.

Abused and misused children will bury feelings, and camouflage them with compliance and dissociation as long as they can. But when life's pressures become too great, or the shame and the pain of recollections surface too sharply (particularly in adolescence with hormones wreaking havoc), rebellion occurs in ways that run the entire gamut, from extreme sadomasochism, to bullying, to nastiness, to murder or suicide. This can happen at home, at work, at school, in places of worship, or in the analyst's office, where it can take the form of trying to kill the analyst with what has been called the 'negative therapeutic reaction.' Quitting treatment precipitously can be seen as homicide and suicide in action.

We analysts build explanatory theories in order to survive the tidal waves of despair. Theories are our life vests, and they *can* be helpful. But, in my mind, one of our best ways to learn is through the enactments that involve projective identifications. Spotting these enactments helps us understand the helplessness, the anxiety, and the rage of our abused patients. It is not unusual when treating a seemingly well put together patient, with a high-level job and the trappings of success to learn years into treatment of childhood abuse. The humiliation suffered is deeply buried but when enough trust develops in the dyad, it feels safe enough to unearth the trauma.

A common enactment of the analyst involves allowing a patient's lateness to go unexplored. The analyst may enjoy the extra time when a patient is late, which may be translated by the patient as "I don't want you here." In this enactment we see a replay of the child and the rejecting mother. The analyst is unconsciously repeating the patient's past. This can happen when the analyst senses that frightening material is in the wings.

Regarding repeated lateness, I have said "Let's figure out what this means." This is an invitation to work together and, if the invitation is made sincerely, with genuine curiosity, a patient is far more likely to respond. This approach also avoids being cast as a nagging mother. The therapist may have an idea that the lateness is a reaction to a separation or a painful session, but it is more important for the patient to wonder. At other times the therapist might say something like, *"I'm wondering if being late is a reaction to my being away?"* A therapist's approach is based on intuition, which is fed by whatever is going on in the dyad (Hall, 1998).

Trying to stop the intergenerational transmission of trauma can seem like trying to stop an avalanche or a run-away freight train. But modification counts, and we must never forget that. It takes a huge amount of time, commitment, courage, and motivation from both parties in the dyad, working in concert, to modify character. The therapist's non-judgmental stance, made possible by the benevolent curiosity that Ella Sharpe (1950) wrote about, along with what Shengold calls *caritas*, and Bion's (1962) idea of *container-contained* fortify the dyad. In my mind, the analyst's major job is clearing the way for the patient to form a new object relationship that will allow her to gradually lay to rest the ghosts that haunt. The plasticity of the brain makes this possible. Doidge (personal communication): "...if you had a bad object relationship with a parent, and now have a better one, the fact that you have a trace of the old one doesn't mean you have to use it." Doidge believes in 'use it or lose it.'

Shengold (1999) said that the essence of psychoanalytic work with someone who has suffered abuse or neglect is

> *"to diminish the power of the link to the internalized, primal destructive parent by enabling the patient to form an*

> *emotional tie with the analyst, and perhaps with others, that is meaningful—a relationship with a separate person, an other who can care and be cared about, love and be loved, without doing physical or emotional harm at the same time."*

I would add that analytic work also allows the good qualities of a "bad" object to surface. That way reparation and forgiveness can occur as the original object representations are softened in the context of a new object to identify with and internalize.

Most of us deal with more camouflaged reactions to the bad enough parent. And yes, other parental objects play an important role in the child's early life, both as support to the mother and as a person who rescues the infant from wishes to merge. Loewald (1951) in his paper "Ego and Reality" speaks of the father as one who rescues the infant from the pull of the maternal womb. He said:

> *"Against the threat of the engulfing, overpowering womb, stands the paternal veto against the libidinal relationship with the mother. Against this threat of the maternal engulfment, the paternal position is not another threat or danger, but a support of powerful force."*

When I read that sentence I pictured a raft that makes swimming away from the shore possible. I also have seen the father take over a maternal role when the mother is unable for whatever reason.

Beneath what we call oedipal guilt we can see early abuse as contributing to what Freud described as those wrecked by success. The same holds true for frigidity and impotence, or inability to form relationships. We see patients who take years to begin to trust. We see past horrors acted out in lives centered on substance abuse, eating disorders, shopping addiction, sadistic and psychopathic behavior, the need to control, phobia, depression, serial marrying, and depression. We see physical symptoms that can become debilitating. We see talent thwarted. We see women and men who cry out for battering and who inflict it on others. Yes, self and soul murder are dramatic terms but I believe that where there is a sadomasochistic character, some degree of self or soul murder has occurred. Psychotherapists can usually see a pattern of maltreatment that goes back several generations. Freud himself was a product of mixed (and narcissistic) mothering and his nanny was said to have been sexually overstimulating and also a thief who was sent to jail. In fact, I wonder along with others, if Freud's phallocentric, oedipal focus served to avoid his separation anxiety sending his mostly male followers down the wrong path. In his time men were expected to be strong and not dependent. Ignoring the woman's role can even be seen as misogynistic. I connect misogyny to disappointment in and fear of the mother.

Try as we therapists do to compete with the bad enough object by offering ourselves as a new object, we sometimes fail and lose hope. This is understandable and not everyone is cut out for such difficult work. It is rarely gratifying and may even be considered as masochistic to try. So those who do hang in deserve appreciation.

Jaak Pankseep's (2012) work shows us that grief is caused by loss. With patients who are able to replace the bad object with what analytic work offers, the light at the end of the tunnel is often a blinding one. In her sixteenth year of four times a week treatment

Lois said she wanted to try twice a week. Usually I see the wish to cut down as a test. *"Are you sure you can stand what's to come?"* is the question—and it is usually rage. So ordinarily I would have protested. I had been schooled to end an analysis in a certain way which did not include tapering off. But by that time in my career I was more interested in what I call patient centered therapy. When the rules we learn become burdens they need re-examining. ONE SIZE DOES NOT FIT ALL. I was aware of my countertransference that was mixed. I was tired. But I was also pleased with the work we had done. Lois had made real strides and so I shared my thoughts with her. By this time our partnership felt secure and as adults, after a long journey, we faced the idea of not only cutting down, but of eventually ending our work. This sharing of ideas proved to be rewarding for both of us. We agreed to twice a week with the option of increasing or of eventual once a week work. If all went well, we would then set a date to say goodbye.

Goodbyes are important milestones in psychoanalytic work. Of course, with certain patients (Oliver Sachs was in analysis for 46 years with Dr. Shengold), treatment lasts a lifetime but if at all feasible, goodbye is an important aim. Why? In my mind the goal of this work is autonomy. It is a wonderful feeling to have achieved enough security to end this demanding work. Standing on one's own two feet is its reward. The connection one develops to the analyst is internalized enabling the work to continue when needed. Analysts have to go through their own mourning and rejoicing but they do that frequently enough and a sense of accomplishment carries both parties through. And even when people leave prematurely, we must know that something has been accomplished. Mr. M's analysis described in *Roadblocks* (Hall, 2003) did not end well—but I think we will always remember each other in a positive way.

Questions

Reflecting back, I wonder if sometimes I expected too much from psychoanalysis—trying to stretch it to include the more damaged patients like Lois. I look back at some of Freud's patients and see that they were not the so-called neurotic. And the more I look around me I see people who function well enough but are carrying private pain. I question the value of too much or ongoing regression in treatment despite Winnicott's work. For some it is necessary and for others it is harmful. On the other hand, when people cross our thresholds we owe them the best that we have to offer and I do believe that depth therapy is most often the answer.

I know too many of us who have been disappointed in our own analyses and yet we continue, in varying degrees, to use the same techniques and theories over and over again. And of course this brings up the Training Analysis question and our educational systems. There are fine Training Analysts but the requirement aspect cannot help but impinge on the process. Gauging what is optimal for a unique patient must be a personal decision and it depends on the unique match (Kantrowitz, 2020). Is our training with its diagnostic approach, and its theories of technique something like putting a square peg in a round hole? Or does it provide a unique holding environment so important when facing pain? If we read the poets of our time—like Anne Carson or Louise Gluck—or see the art of our time that breaks boundaries—and if we are open to the "new"—should we analysts break free from our conservative beliefs? And if so, how much? My training was orthodox, yet over the years I have seen both its upsides and its downsides. Is there another way to educate students? Hopefully we know that institute learning is only the beginning.

I chose the title of this book, *The Power of Connection,* well aware that connecting is often a slow process. But if we therapists are patient and courageous, connection can happen. And only when it does will self-murder gives way to self-birth. Two people take a journey during which new growth occurs and although the travel can be exhausting the rewards make it well worth it.

CHAPTER 4

RIFF: PUT ON YOUR THERAPY HAT

Before you open your office door to greet your patient, take a moment to center yourselves. (Put on your therapy hat.)

Take a deep breath and remember who you are at that very moment.

Remember how you got where you are.

Remember that you have studied, you have had or are in supervision, you have experienced or are experiencing your own psychoanalytic work. You will be the professional in the room, and if this is your first patient, you will be taking the first steps on your real learning curve.

Remember that you are not omniscient and that there are no answers, just possibilities and options.

Convey to your patient, in your own natural way, that you are willing and able to listen and that when you begin to understand or have an idea, you will share that understanding or offer that idea for contemplation and conversation.

Convey that this is mutual work at understanding and that it will promote growth and change.

If the patient is experiencing panic, suicidal ideation, or unbearable pain, act accordingly. Ask the patient to be with someone she trusts. Discuss hospitalization and local ERs. Suggest meeting the following day. Remember, you are a psychoanalytically oriented clinician, an explorer, and not an ER doctor.

Know that each patient, in each hour will teach you something new. Your ears, your senses, and your intuition will enable you to tune in and that tuning in is your biggest gift. In return, you will gain your patient's trust as you embark on a most intriguing journey with your partner.

Those readers who know me or have read my books, know that my favorite phrase is *benevolent curiosity*. If you were not curious you would not be reading this book. Genuine, benevolent curiosity is contagious. Sometimes, however, it takes years for a patient to tell you their secrets. These secrets have caused shame which can feel unbearable. If you pass the tests along the way, and there will be many, your patient will give you clues and will eventually tell you their secrets. (In the third year of therapy a patient told me of her 'alters'—her other selves (Hall, 2003).

For me, genuine respect for the patient, conviction in the value of psychoanalytic work along with benevolent curiosity are the keys that opens all doors. All the real knowledge you and your patient gain comes from your ability to be hopeful and to be curious. As time goes on, your patients will begin using those keys—and when that happens the work is well on its way. When the patient ceases to be her own worst critic and shifts to wanting to know "why," your alliance will carry you through to the end. Of course, along the way, old patterns of mistrust, hatred, rage, will appear. But, these moments or periods will not frighten or intimidate you. You and your partner will have developed the strength necessary to stay afloat and to weather the inevitable storms.

The very first meeting between patient and therapist sets the stage for what's to come. A warm, concerned, professional demeanor, unlike the stiff classical stereotypical analyst of the old days, leaves an indelible impression. We often take this for granted but I have heard feedback from patients years later about how meaningful those first moments were. It is our own comfort and conviction that sets the stage for work. Sometimes we clinicians are taught to be neutral and a bit removed. At one time abstinence included not smiling or shaking hands. Some of you may have experienced analysts as a bit less than real, so be real. Be yourself. Don't put on airs. I do not mean that we grin, chew gum, or behave super casually. But we must be welcoming, gracious, with the aim of providing as comfortable an experience as possible. This attitude must be naturally conveyed.

So, sit back and mentally lean in.

CHAPTER 5

MASOCHISM & PATIENCE

My heart is sad and lonely
For you I sigh, for you, dear, only
Why haven't you seen it?
I'm all for you, body and soul

I spend my days in longin'
And wond'ring why it's me you're wrongin'
I tell you, I mean it
I'm all for you, body and soul

I can't believe it, it's hard to conceive it
That you'd turn away romance
Are you pretending? It looks like the ending
Unless I could have one more chance to prove, dear

My life a wreck you're making
You know I'm yours for just the taking
I'd gladly surrender
Myself to you, body and soul
—Edward Heyman, Robert Sour and Frank Eyton,
Body and Soul

Fools rush in, so here I am
Very glad to be unhappy
I can't win, but here I am
More than glad to be unhappy
Unrequited love's a bore
And I've got it pretty bad
But for someone you adore
It's a pleasure to be sad
— Rogers and Hart,
Glad to Be Unhappy

Life often seems unfair but recognizing that we cannot change certain things can be even more painful than the unfairness. It is a long fall from what we imagine to be the infant's feelings of omnipotence to the reality of its helplessness. To ease the pain the child normally uses magical thinking that is eventually replaced to varying degrees by the reality principle. Psychoanalysts believe that fantasy life often lives underground in the unconscious where it maintains great influence on the adult and also offers a retreat when reality becomes unbearable. If we think about it, we spend our lives warding off the inevitable. The worlds of advertising along with Hollywood and Bollywood, the porn business, the entire entertainment industry all perpetuate magical thinking with promises of nirvana, omniscience, and everlasting youth. Not only can Superman fly, he also does not age. And, what we call perversion and even corruption make sense when we see their birthplaces: early childhood trauma.

It isn't easy to leave the womb, and depending on our genes and our first experiences with our first caretakers, life unfolds in unique ways. Whereas Freud focused on the closed system of drives, instincts, id, ego, superego, the topographic theory, the death instinct, he left little room for outside influences. Today we recognize outside influences that cannot help but affect who we are. Being poor can create any of the following conditions: lack of food, inferior food, polluted water, poor or no shelter, and lack of opportunity that affect the child directly. His parents' frustrations and anxieties surely compromise the quality of caretaking. Extreme wealth may cause different problems as illustrated in Chapter Three, Self-Murder. Loss and illness have devastating effects as do hurricanes and tornadoes.

All the more reason, one would think, to find as much enjoyment as reasonably and legally (or not) possible. So, when faced with masochistic behavior we are at a loss. Why would someone choose a life of suffering. Psychoanalysts from Freud to the present have been pondering this question and have come up with all sorts of reasons and theories that include the death drive, guilt, aggression, revenge, defense, perversion, trauma, genetics, brain abnormalities and more. We may accept all these theories but how do they help the clinician when faced with a masochistic patient. Beyond the theories how do we help those who persist in harming themselves and others (sadism is really the opposite side of the same coin and it is not difficult to see how the masochist tortures others.) I have chosen to look at this dilemma through a developmental lens. The following ideas are speculative and I offer them as possibilities.

Childhood is filled with calamities often bordering on and including physical and/or emotional abuse. Losing a parent, being hated by a parent, being treated as an extension of a parent, being betrayed or abandoned by a parent, being constantly criticized or punished, and receiving mixed messages from a parent are unfortunately common injustices. The statistics on child abuse show that it is far more common than we like to realize. These statistics, however, do not include the emotional abuse that most of our patients have suffered and continue to suffer as adults. The emotionally abused child buys into her plight because she believes her mother who calls her names, criticizes, demeans, or ignores her. He believes his father who beats him without mercy. The first self that such a child constructs is based on parental opinions which become their opinion, even as they protest. This is one template registered in the brain and unless there are other important, beloved figures who counter the mother's message, she will miss out on the self-esteem which is crucial to healthy development.

Jill was seen by her therapist as a masochist. She was always setting herself up to be hurt, demeaned, and taken advantage of, both emotionally and even physically. The therapist had learned from reading Freud that masochism is caused by unconscious guilt stemming from the oedipus complex. This guided her listening. She interpreted Jill's choice of unavailable, hard-to-please, even abusive male partners as a fear of having a man all to herself which would be experienced, in fantasy, as an oedipal victory thus bringing on even more of mother's wrath. It is this guilt according to Freud and Jill's therapist that caused her to choose unavailable, unkind, or narcissistic men who made her feel inadequate by rejecting her. The rejections further embedded Jill's belief that she was flawed and therefore undeserving. Jill was aware that she set herself up for disappointment and came to therapy to find out why.

The oedipal interpretation did not help matters. Why? Because the therapist was using a particular theory to influence her impressions, and so she missed Jill's references to her earliest experience with a mother who continuously and severely criticized her. It was this criticism and Jill's longing for her mother's love that needed attention. Jill's unconscious quest in life was to change the situation by earning her narcissistic mother's love and acceptance. I propose that her hope came from the grandiose days of magical thinking that warded off depression and perhaps a retreat to psychosis. The men she chose actually represented her rejecting mother from whom she had never fully separated. She thought that by acquiescing to a man's every need she could gain his love which unconsciously equated to her mother's love. Jill's choices in friends and mates were based on replicating the original bond to mother. By appearing to be pathetic she protected herself from mother's envy and further cruelty. But it was the cruelty of rejection that she also craved because it was familiar and therefore safe. A brain scientist might see all this as reinforcing the original neural pathways that perpetuated Jill's experience by affecting her perception. How? If Jill registered her mother's opinion before individuation had been firm enough, that opinion becomes her truth. Jill perceived herself as defective while at the same time denying the idea.

In my view it was not oedipal guilt that caused Jill to find punishing objects. Instead it was Jill's relationship with mother that needed attention. Jill was seeking critical and unavailable men in order to maintain a relationship she did not have the strength to give up.

An unavailable or hostile mother figure makes it frightening for the child to separate and individuate.

We might conclude that on an unconscious level, Jill was stuck somewhere in the separation-individuation phase and in order to continue her development she needed the encouragement from a good-enough rapprochement mother. Research (Knight, 2021) shows that separation individuation is an ongoing process and not limited to early childhood so treatment provides an opportunity to get normal development back on track.

The child's thrust to individuate, when successful, provides the self-esteem necessary to move on. Jill's attachment to abuse was based on her attachment to mother and until she developed self-esteem elsewhere, she felt stuck. Developmentally speaking, it appeared that she had not differentiated self and object sufficiently. I believe this is a basic dilemma of many self harming individuals who, while hurting themselves are also harming the undifferentiated object in their representational world.

This is where the therapist can help, and depending on the severity of the problem, it can be an arduous task requiring much patience. Ego building techniques are called for and this approach requires the analyst's creativity and ingenuity. Why? Because Jill had been brainwashed into believing that she was defective. After all, who would know her better than mother, and challenging or ignoring mother's opinion meant losing her on an unconscious level. As she grew up this view of herself that coincided with mother's view colored all relationships and most importantly strengthened the bond with her mother imago. It is that early representation (neural pathway in the brain) that is so hard to change, and it may, in fact, be unchangeable. Jill needed to find other experiences but this was not easy. Why? I think it is because this early relationship is foundational and it has the power to skew perception. Jill actually perceived herself as unworthy and undeserving despite her obvious successes. Interestingly, development in some areas seems to proceed despite failing in other areas and this is confusing to say the least. Many successful people have differentiation issues.

When viewed this way, the therapist's role must shift from defense analysis to ego building and from interpretation to explanation along with validation of the patient's remembered experience. This does not mean that the therapist should start complimenting Jill. Instead she must find ways to allow Jill to see and experience her own strength, even if it just involves coming to therapy. We analysts tend to forget the courage it takes for a person to call for and to keep an appointment.

One day Jill was a few minutes late and mentioned a meeting at work where her idea about a new ad campaign had been applauded. The therapist wanted to hear the details but Jill changed the subject, complaining about traffic.

> *Therapist: Let's talk about why you changed the subject. It feels like you don't want to tell me about it.*
>
> *Jill: (silent for a few minutes) you aren't really interested.*
>
> *Therapist: Well, the fact is that I am but what we need to figure out is why you would imagine that I wouldn't be interested. (this*

is an invitation to work together which is ego building. In effect the therapist is asking for Jill's input instead of interpreting her transference.)

Jill begins to reminisce about her mom's disinterest giving examples of her cruelty. The dyad talked about how a child needs encouragement, and this led to a conversation about her adorable three-year-old god-daughter whose mom was so great.

Jill: I wish I'd had a mom like that.

In her next session Jill repeated her fear that the therapist was like her critical mother which gave the therapist an opportunity to talk about the tendency we all have to experience present relationships based on the past.

Therapist: I totally understand why you imagine that I would be like your mom. I'm probably about her age and as your therapist I fit into that parent mold. Also, we all use the past to predict the future. Actually it makes perfect sense, but as we become adults we realize that people are different and we fight the tendency to let the past influence our opinions.

Here the therapist is explaining why we experience transference and even what we do about it, while stepping aside to ally herself with her partner. She takes care not to blame Jill or her mother, but let's Jill entertain this new idea. It may sound intellectual but the conversation continued for several sessions and one day Jill began to cry. The realization that her mother was an unhappy woman with her own problems that she took out on Jill brought forth the emotions Jill had been holding in for a very long time.

These explanations allowed Jill to begin forming a new relationship with the therapist who serves as self-object and ally (Kohut, 1971; Berliner, 1958; Loewald, 1960). The analyst's attitude does not include pity or insincere commiseration. It means matter-of-fact acknowledgement of the difficulties Jill experienced. It required many long conversations because separating from mother is not easy.

> *Therapist: Jill, it sounds like your mother's constant criticism screwed you up and even if she couldn't help it, we need to figure out what to do about it.*

Of course, this is easier said than done but it plants a seed of hope. It also let's Jill know she has an ally.

Seeing adult patients who continue to expose themselves to injustice is frustrating for the therapist. A masochistic patient can be extremely hard to sit with. Time after time she will find herself attached and attracted to people who treat her poorly. Sometimes she treats her self poorly as in eating disorders or drug use or even self cutting. Suicide can be seen as killing self and object. Although Jill complained about being treated badly, she sought out and held on to maltreatment in an unconscious attempt to hold onto mother, while at the same time hoping to change her. But nothing works until differentiation is accomplished, and even when it is, I see it as fluid. The freedom to explore the world is contingent on having the mother's encouragement and by returning to her when necessary. All this works together to allow the child's recognition of separateness.

Sue was in love with a 'hard-to-get' man. He was not interested in marriage having witnessed his parents divorce and all that led up to it. But after three years of living together he proposed to Sue and after the wedding she actually experienced euphoria, or was it elation. She felt as though she was literally walking without touching the ground on the way home from the wedding. It was as if a huge weight had been lifted, the weight of a life long rejection. In her analysis she came to see that her elation had to do with the idea of finally winning her husband/mother's love. Of course the elation didn't last. When she came down to earth she began experiencing bouts of rage that she directed at her husband. A normal disagreement would escalate into a screaming match at which point her husband would leave the house. Sue's intense separation anxiety took hold and she offered profuse apologies even though she couldn't remember what she had done. She seemed completely unaware of her outbursts. Even when reminded of the issues she had screamed about, she could not remember. As with Lois in Chapter Three it was as if a split off self-state suddenly came on stage. Sue's analytic work helped her realize that the real source of the elation and anger stemmed from childhood with a screaming mother who continuously made it clear that she had never wanted a child. On some level Sue's husband represented her mother so that while winning his love was elating it also brought forth her rage. Because differentiation, when not completed enough, means some degree of fusion of self and object, rage that is expressed to the object is also injurious to the self. This is my idea of sadomasochism, a blend of the raw rage of disappointment and intense needy love.

Sue's analysis eventually helped her relinquish this hope for mother's approval as she developed her own sense of self. It took many years to realize that she was not the "piece of shit" her mother said she was. The developmental step of forming a self apart from mother was finally accomplished after years of hard work that included internalizing the analytic work. Sue and her analyst knew that there would always be a scar but, as with most scars, it would become barely noticeable.

Blending theory is risky but I shall try. As the original neural pathway representing mother and daughter was diminishing, other pathways representing experiences with the analyst as new object became available. It is thought that the hormone oxytocin (the love hormone) stimulates this process.

Normal development gets derailed when a child falters in the separation individuation phase. Lack of sufficiently differentiated self and object means degrees of fusion with mother. Sue was stuck with mother's message and until the therapist is cathected (invested with positive emotions like love) this child/adult will continue the familiar sadomasochistic dance. She will repeatedly evoke maltreatment because she has no choice. Even the material she brought to therapy was frustrating to the therapist who struggled to stay connected without succumbing to the patient's attempts to cast her as the original object. This view fits the neural pathway explanation that neuroscientists propose. Using the same pathway over and over makes it more difficult to hear and to register other messages. It is akin to brainwashing. I once had a patient who actually did not hear compliments and was always blaming her husband for not appreciating her. When he insisted that she listen to his expressions of appreciation, she didn't believe him or said they were not enough. This is like what Newell Fischer (2019) termed malabsorption disease. Those who were seriously deprived of love seem allergic after a certain point.

In many instances early caretakers have been abusive, intrusive, neglectful, and narcissistic. These early figures and their actions are registered by the mind and brain (internalized) affecting the child's perception and coloring its future perceptions. In therapy the patient is presented with a new object with whom to identify and gradually internalize. As Sue began to separate from her original object, perceptions that had been black and white and one dimensional expanded into colorful multidimensionality. The development of ambivalence (holding opposing feelings at the same time) increased reality testing so that her perspective broadened. Lisa in Chapter Nine, towards the end of analysis said that she had developed a new sense of color and shape never experienced before and we wondered if different neural pathways had became available.

Another way of saying all this is that as a false self fades, a person becomes unburdened by the need to please. Self esteem builds as the ego strengthens and the superego loses its harshness. As stress diminishes the body chemistry changes and symptoms abate. The analytic process of connection with a new object (therapist) is thought to occur when the hormone oxytocin is released due to the positive and even erotic transference. I recently witnessed work with a patient whose serious, life threatening physical symptoms that stumped over ten doctors, recover completely during her analysis. This particular patient had felt completely neglected as a child and adolescent and her body literally screamed out for attention.

As differentiation proceeds, repeating the past is no longer necessary and moving forward is possible. The loving aspects of the self, originally shaded over by early trauma, become available, enabling recognition of the analyst and then others as separate and different. Brain researchers say "The brain you go to sleep with is always different than the one you wake up with!" The years spent in analysis have to change the brain.

The human brain is made up of an estimated 100 billion neurons making a total of 100 trillion neural connections. It is possible that with new emotional connections, new pathways can be found that lead to change.

I realize that all this may have been hard to follow because it's like trying to speak three languages at the same time (brain-speak, chemistry, and psychological development.) And I realize that these ideas are complex and that some are speculative. But I do think that analysts must avail themselves of the findings that scientific research is providing. It is difficult to blend theory but it seems worth the effort.

But without the theory, perhaps all this can happen naturally. Perhaps the patient's motivation, fed by newly gained self-esteem due to the analyst's concern, with a strengthened ego will permit Jill, Sue, and others to rid themselves of the old defective self-image (tie to the mother/brain pathway) thereby allowing them to choose new and available love partners. As we gain new experiences, some connections are strengthened while others fade. This process is known as synaptic pruning. Many analysts refuse to think that neuroscience has anything to offer psychoanalysis, but why? Is this the close-mindedness that I find dangerous? To me it's like a writer refusing to learn to use a computer.

If the child has managed to extract something good, something positive along the way, this in itself can lay down separate neural pathways that can be used as the tie to the bad enough mother weakens. When a newborn is held and fed, as the brain is developing, these neural pathways are there for future use.

The problem is that masochism takes on a sense of power due to the once normal omnipotent phase of development and this complicates the issue. Theoretically, we also see this power as the opposite side of the coin which is sadism. An adult patient may feel pleasure in defeating the therapist as mother in the transference by continuing her suffering and so the stakes grow higher. I think it is important to realize how very complicated the mind is and to respect this fact. The term resistance comes to mind. The idea of overcoming resistance through interpretation makes little sense when considering a patient's developmental phase. Reluctance to give up the pleasure of safety is understandable (remember, safety can contain pain) so as the dyad connects, the original unconscious reluctance diminishes because a new sense of safety is available. It takes strength to move ahead and in my mind, if the analyst recognizes this, the term resistance has no place. Even the word reluctance when referring to issues of trust, seems wrong. Trust must be earned. My focus is on the power of connection. I think therapists must be careful not to buy into Freud's pessimism. We must be able to appreciate even small gains and our appreciation is picked up by the patient unconsciously. Cure is not our goal. Allowing development to proceed towards the achievement of autonomy is our job.

I believe that most people experience sadomasochism to one degree or another, at one time or another, and it may even be a part of human nature. For our purposes however, suffering may bring much needed attention; it may ward off attack and envy; it may assuage a punishing superego; and it may be a defense against psychosis. There is a wide spectrum of causes and effects to consider including genetics, epigenetics, and the intergenerational transmission of trauma. So, we therapists must respect the uniqueness of our patients. Our theories are like condiments used in making a stew, to be used carefully. Think of a musical chord like A minor 7th with a flatted ninth—all the notes contribute to the sound.

My ideas stem from a developmental approach which is only one of many ways to think about sadomasochism. We must remember that a normal omnipotent phase of development feeds into the fantasy of altering reality and that reality itself is relative. A two year old's reality is far different from a twelve year old's.

If there are no positive relationships to offset the mother's destructive messages, or if her messages were accompanied by physical harm, the child may retreat to her fantasy world which further prevents her from allowing new experiences in. By the way, how many of us adults knock on wood or cross our fingers, both remnants of magical omnipotence that is deeply embedded in our brains.

Another aspect to consider: masochism can be seen as anger directed towards the self. Psychosomatic illness, accident proneness, even attempts to kill oneself can be seen as desperate calls for help. The severity of these symptoms may indicate the degree of childhood abuse suffered. The complexities of this issue are reflected by the many psychoanalytic theories dedicated to understanding it. What is the masochist saying to herself through self destructive behavior: *"You idiot! If you had been perfect she would love you so now you deserve punishment."* If self and object are fused, both suffer.

It is incomprehensible to a young child that the abuse she suffers has nothing to do with her because of her normal feelings of omnipotence, primary narcissism, and magical thinking. One patient remembered the childhood rituals he performed, believing he could control the frightening screams he heard from his parents' room. If he put his toys in a certain position the noise would stop and he would be safe. This was the beginning of his obsessive-compulsive character style.

We therapists must remember that a child's feelings of omnipotence are normal and subside slowly with individuation and the recognition of the other; so until this has been accomplished it is quite understandable that a masochistic patient believes that he can change things by suffering. As an adult he may intellectually recognize this truth yet the fantasy lingers on. *"If I can live up to her expectations she'll marry me"* said a masochistic patient. The statement held out hope as it had when being berated by an alcoholic father or screamed at by an out of control mother. The fact that this patient could not have any influence on a beloved person was even more painful than the maltreatment itself. It requires many years of analytic work for such a patient to recognize and then to let go of this fantasy that becomes deeply engraved in one's psyche. Piaget (1929) said that magical thinking is most prominent in children between ages 2 and 7. Due to examinations of grieving children, it is said that during this age, children strongly believe that their personal thoughts have a direct effect on the rest of the world. It is posited that their minds will create a reason to feel responsible if they experience something tragic that they do not understand.

Even without developmental theory we know that a mother's love, encouragement, and approval matter tremendously to her child. Accepting the flaws of one's parents and of oneself requires mourning the loss of omnipotence. The undercurrent of love in the analytic dyad cushions the pain, making it bearable.

Anna grew up a neglected child. Her mother was a lawyer with a full practice and her dad was always traveling for work. She was cared for by a series of incompetent nannies. Anna's parents expected her to excel at school and when she didn't they punished her with their disdain. When she finished college she married a classmate who was withdrawn and needy. She grudgingly tolerated his behavior that seemed to stem from an autistic disorder. Anna sought therapy due to her increasing depression and after three years she had a good job and was established in her career. But her husband continued to be demanding and stubborn so therapy centered around his refusal, or perhaps inability to change. Did he represent her on some level? The therapist became frustrated because Anna, despite her achievements refused to go ahead with her plans to divorce him.

Sessions were filled with her complaints about him. The therapist was angry and felt stymied. Was Anna's therapist picking up on Anna's dilemma through projective identification? Situations like this are indeed frustrating so what can the therapist do?

First of all I suggest stepping back and reviewing where the masochistic patient got stuck in her development. Clues can be found in the history. Was there a sick child needing attention? Was the mother depressed? Were other siblings helpful or did they torture the patient? Was the patient sickly? Why was she spinning her wheels in the rut created in her childhood? Where in her separation/individuation phase did she falter or fail? I have seen that the rapprochement phase—where the toddler explores the world away from the mother but refuels by going back or looking back in order to feel secure—if faulty causes fears of moving on. Such children often grow up with phobias and extreme shyness. They need the mother figure to ground them, even when pain is involved. Lacking the mother's permission and encouragement to move ahead in life, these children develop intense separation and sometimes annihilation anxiety. In Anna's case leaving her husband was too frightening. Knowing that he was there was more important than any joy she missed. Did the husband who did love her through his neediness represent her and her need for a good mother? Did he represent a mother who was always there? And did Anna unconsciously believe that if she let go of mother/husband they would die or she would die? Could her need/rage kill them? Did she fear devouring them? Then what would she do?

One day Anna talked about stopping therapy. After encouraging her to explore why, she said: *"I'm failing here and you are getting fed up with me."* Her therapist answered: *"Anna, could it be that you imagine me as being like your mom who expected so much from you?"* Anna cried and finally agreed that she feared being rejected once again. This opened up a conversation about separation anxiety. They connected it to Anna's difficulty ending her sessions and how she would linger by the door with questions or chatter. The therapist understood the calls between sessions in a different light. She decided to answer some of Anna's questions before her vacation and as they talked about where she was going a new closeness developed. Anna felt stronger and because she felt she was being treated as an adult, her self-esteem grew and her object-constancy improved. (Therapists must remember not to infantilize their patients which is tricky because of their regressions.) Exploring this anxiety helped Anna trace it to its source which had to do with her hidden anger at her mother and fears that something bad would happen because of them. Memories of fearing school and going to camp were eventually connected to separating from her mother and then to leaving her husband. She could begin to see that they also represented her and that she expected them to feel abandoned. There were so many things to consider and talking about them strengthened the therapeutic bond. This might be seen as intellectualizing but as I've said, the intellect is an ego strength that can prepare one for emotional understanding.

In my experience it takes incredible patience and understanding to work with a masochistic character. Such patients unconsciously fear losing a steady object for myriad reasons as just discussed. Getting better often threatens them with thoughts of losing the therapist. So depending on the unique patient I recommend explaining the predicament over time. Conversation that includes what it would be like without the husband can help. But patience and ego building techniques are necessary. Understanding how upsetting a patient's early memories are help the analyst stay connected. Here's where self-disclosure may be appropriate:

> *Therapist: Anna, I can hardly imagine how that felt—it reminds me of a time when I got lost in a department store and couldn't find my mother. I was about four and I was so scared. All the people were so tall, I couldn't see their faces and it was awful.*

Actually, the impatience felt by the therapist can be a reaction to the patient's sadism. The refusal to change is not just due to the patient's inability—it is also an expression of her anger—like stubbornly digging one's heels in. Remember the power of the two-year-old's *NO!* Also, we think of projective identification meaning that the patient projects her dilemma on to the therapist who learns just how helpless her patient felt and still feels.

Change can take many years of painful work on both sides of the couch and therapists must sometimes struggle to stay involved. This is where benevolent curiosity can save the day. The therapist might say something like: *"Let's figure out why you can't seem to let go of this painful position"* which illustrates her non-judgmental curiosity and her invitation to work side by side. It does no good to reason with or encourage the patient to take action. Suggestions and even encouragement from the therapist are ignored and this is where we see must wonder if the patient is unable to move on or whether she is being sadistic, or both. Many of us talk about the negative therapeutic reaction which is too speculative for me. If a patient refuses our help maybe we should look at how we're offering it. I used to teach a paper called "Attachment to Painful Negative Feelings" (Valenstein, 1973) about a young man who was said to have a negative therapeutic reaction. The analyst made a compelling argument but as I reread it over the years, I began to question his technique. Sometimes if we ask a patient what we're doing wrong in a sincere manner, the patient will tell us.

Sometimes during a treatment we begin to feel useless and even trampled upon (projective identification and the patient's sadism). What saves us is our realization that we are being made to feel the way our patient feels, powerless and powerful at the same time. Here is where the deepening comes in, slowly and often imperceptibly. Even as we begin to feel victimized by a patient, our patient starts to notice that we can sit with her while taking care of ourselves at the same time. We set boundaries. We might say something like: *"Anna, I think you are trying to let me know how you felt as a child—that whatever you did it was not good enough."* or *"I wonder what it was like to come home to an empty house day after day. Only when you were sick or injured did your mom pay attention."* Such observations hopefully encourage the patient to continue talking.

Expecting to be paid on time, raising fees when appropriate, charging for missed sessions, holding to the schedule, looking well, feeling well, enjoying our lives are ways to let our patients experience that we have tamed our own sadomasochistic tendencies. One way or another we manage to stay, to do the work. In fact a therapist's staying power is what reaches the patient more than we often realize. But staying may be felt as masochistic by the therapist and when it does it may be best to level with the partner. Something like: *"Anna, we have been working for years and nothing seems to help. I am feeling quite useless to you and I think we should figure out what to do. What are your thoughts?"* Enlisting the patient's observing ego is helpful in such situations. Our appeal tells a patient that we respect her thoughts which is quite unlike making an interpretation. We must also realize that the patient has been surviving with this character solution for a long time and may not let it go until she feels sure of the analyst's love. We must remember that at one time masochism was Anna's only avenue of hope. If she brought punishment on herself, she was really in control.

Our psychoanalytic studies can take us only so far. Each of us and each of our patients are unique as are our struggles together. We must learn that it's ok to trust our intuition and to be receptive to theirs. Our theories are the scaffolding that, once internalized, free us to improvise. Learning many theories is like learning the scales in many keys for the musician, but our own personalities always determine how we use them. Sometimes we become passionate—exhorting our masochistic patient to speak up in an unfair situation. Now, of course this does not work, but part of the message may give our patient a glimpse of what it looks like to fight back. Remaining neutral is not always possible or even positive. With Anna I might have said at some point *"Anna, I think I would really lose my temper if he treated me that way."* Or *"Anna, I think you realize that John cannot change—no matter what you do and it may be hard to let that sink in. It reminds me of how hard you tried to please your parents—to no avail. But in my experience, the pain of letting go diminishes as one lets new experiences in."*

What Happens that Allows Change?

Being loved and loving is complicated. But the complexity of love allows us to understand how important a life force it is and shows us that people have unique ways of keeping it alive even as they seem to push it away. Some people feel that their love must be hidden and this deprives them of full connection. I feel that conversation leads to connection and I advocate talking with the patient instead of delivering wise interpretations. When connecting feels dangerous to a patient, it means that development was dangerous. I think that analytic work seeks to remove barriers that have impeded development with what Shengold called caritas. This is what sets development back on track. Seeing that the analyst stays in all kinds of emotional weather reaches the patient who begins to feel worthwhile. She feels the analyst's caritas which builds the self esteem needed for growth. During the process both parties will feel hopeless at times because of the patient's fear of loss which often takes the form of what looks like stubborn refusal to move ahead. So it is helpful to remember how dangerous change feels to the patient.

One aspect of masochistic behavior is an attempt to ward off abandonment. Pain whether mental or physical provides connection. Even self inflicted pain involves a fantasy of being rescued. Years of therapy are usually required for it takes time to feel safe, to mourn loss, and to develop new ways of relating. Change usually happens so slowly that we sometimes don't notice. I remember being criticized for my twenty-two year work with Lisa (Chapter Ten) but we both felt success and I learned that those years were necessary. What's really going on is development that had been derailed.

Anna began losing weight which she did on her own, making her quite attractive and one day a co-worker began to flirt with her. This increased her self-esteem which made letting go of her marriage seem doable. Losing weight was something she did so it meant that she felt ready to move on. I believe that she also sensed my respect.

Psychoanalytic work is concerned with providing a space for development to get back on track when it has been derailed just as much as it is for conflict resolution. In fact, I wonder if many analyses of the so-called neurotic, featuring interpretation of the infantile neurosis, are enabling development to proceed without the analyst framing it in these terms. As Anna got stronger she proceeded with the task of individuating. Being a separate individual meant being able to let go of a destructive mother representation, a mother she finally felt strong enough to do without.

A masochistic attitude is always linked to the past and it is hard to let go of. Why? Probably for as many reasons as there are theories and then some. An important one, discussed above, has to do with development and its connection to the brain's neural pathways that get stronger with use. I think that the mind's capacities to create symptoms, both physical and mental, grow from trauma. Whatever hormones are excreted must play a big role in the brain's circuitry. (If I were younger this is the area I'd devote time to.)

During adolescence the pain of unrequited love can mask the separation anxiety of growing up and leaving childhood. When patients see and experience the therapist's strength in tolerating their grief and anxiety without judging or threatening or criticizing them, they are exposed to and faced with another way of being. This way of being is new and patients try hard to reject it because what's familiar feels safe!

My patient Ellen would get so anxious about exposing her deep rage that she would begin to leave the session early. Her leg would begin to shake and she was visibly upset. One day as she reached the door I said firmly: *"Ellen, sit down. It is really important for you to stay."* She was testing me to see whether I could tolerate her and whether we could tolerate her rage. She had tested me many times in different ways before. She needed to see that I was not afraid or helpless. Her own shame was unbearable to her, but not to me. After two years she started to face the abuse she was so ashamed of and the anger she had hidden. Abuse and the anger it causes is familiar and hard to let go of—but it happens slowly and patience is a therapist's biggest ally. Some patients actually succeed in upsetting the therapist who either wishes to retaliate or even to give up. This is when consultation really helps. This work can be extremely difficult especially when the transference is allowed to intensify. This is when I suggest reminding the patient that we are allies in a tough battle.

Many if not most patients test the therapist. This is absolutely appropriate and I consider this an ego strength. I believe that our ability to maintain our composure no matter what, is crucial. This does not mean that sometimes we don't lose it. We are human and particularly when we are distracted by our own problems we err. I have even forgotten an appointment. There is nothing wrong with apologizing when appropriate, in fact genuine apologies set a good example.

In sum, the masochistic patient, like any patient, requires patience and benevolent curiosity. We must remember that there are many reasons that one allows oneself or even asks to be injured and it is our job to explore these reasons. We work together to figure it out.

Sadomasochistic relationships are not unusual. What often happens is that a couple takes turns punishing each other in very subtle or obvious ways. Who has the power is the game. What goes into the need for power is worthy of at least another twenty books but I suspect that some sort of abuse was involved.

I end this chapter reluctantly because this is a fascinating subject, but I hope I have stimulated the reader to explore it and to remember that benevolent curiosity can save the day. Asking "Why" with genuine sincerity has pulled me through some very tough spots.

CHAPTER 6

RICHARD

"Goodnight sweet Prince"
— Shakespeare, *Hamlet*

In 1972, Richard, a 28-year-old, successful, gay designer was mandated by the court to get therapy in order to avoid jail time after being arrested for "lewd" sex in a public bathroom. He was referred to the Greenwich House Counseling Center where he began once-a-week therapy with me. When I opened my private practice he chose to come with me and began a three- and eventually five-times-a-week psychoanalysis. I had not yet graduated from the institute where couch and frequency were requirements in the practice of psychoanalysis. By the time I graduated I was seeing four people in five-times-a-week treatment. It just seemed natural to me, and my conviction was picked up by my patients. I remember telling each of them that analysis was, in my opinion, the treatment of choice, and that it offered the best way to achieve their goals. Three of the four benefitted, and one ended prematurely.

Memories of childhood suggested that Richard felt glued to his mother as though he were her double, her twin—or her. She treated him as a part of herself and began the killing of them both with her drug use and her seductive behavior. As an adult, that behavior became his behavior as he calmed his anxiety with her drug of choice, Placydil (switching later to Valium) and then, turning to amphetamines to give him the energy he needed to keep, in fantasy, her adoration. The anger he buried often threatened his successful career for it was expressed in the form of procrastination. He would promise and then not deliver. We had many conversations about this and, by realizing the source of the behavior, it slowly lost its attraction.

Richard began expressing his anger with words instead of actions. His aggression provided the fuel he needed to separate and to become his own self. This is why I feel that intellectual understanding, often frowned upon by psychoanalysts, can actually help. Structurally speaking, when a patient realizes that he was powerless as a child, it assuages the punitive superego thereby fortifying the ego with the strength needed for individuation. At least this happened with Richard. As he recognized that as a child he was helpless in dealing with his mother's anxiety, it sank in and he became less flamboyant and took himself more seriously. Such a process may even allow reparations with past objects and to objects in the internal world. Why? Because as the patient gains new perspective the past seems less toxic. Empathy may develop for both self and object. Some patients become psychologically minded and choose to continue their development by becoming psychotherapists. Identification with the therapist is understandable and hopefully this leads to even more individuation. Although some will argue that intellectual knowledge is superficial as it does not reach the unconscious, I have not seen proof of that reasoning. As powerful as the unconscious is, I have seen that knowledge is also a potent weapon.

Richard was ashamed of his feminine mannerisms and at times he spitefully exaggerated them. He taunted, seduced, agonized, performed, and finally cried out his disgust with his past and the despair he felt. Years went by as he slowly grew to trust me and our work. Gradually he developed his own sense of self and formed a relationship with a significant other, but it was too late. Promiscuous, anonymous, unprotected sex had, early on, been his attempt to replace the intimacy he had so feared. He was one of the first to die from complications of AIDS, his life a long-drawn-out homicide/suicide. I dedicate this chapter to him.

Richard teased me from the start. In his first year of therapy. He brought me a chocolate-covered tool kit for Valentine's Day, and when I asked about this gift he said he wanted me to fix him. He entertained me, even secretly followed me, (this was before the internet) trying to learn about me. His mother had done the same to him. She actually moved into an apartment across from his so she could spy and catch glimpses of his wealthy and famous clients.

I originally thought about his spying as voyeurism which I had learned at the institute was a perversion. As I came to learn more, I challenged this thinking and connected it to his intense separation anxiety. He needed to keep me in sight and to know everything about me. Yes, this was sexualized and took on other meanings but the original fear of separating lay at the core. As I understood it, Richard did not have the strength necessary to differentiate from his narcissistic, needy mother who saw him as an extension of herself. Individuating was part of our work. But first we had to connect. As we worked, and as he slowly came to trust me, his self-esteem began to increase. Richard became able to own his success in a new way. Before treatment he had split off his professional life, and it seemed to belong to someone else. Accepting this "self-state" or part of himself provided the fuel he needed to separate. One day, when showing me a magazine article about his work, he said, in a tone of dawning awareness: "*I really did that!*"

Richard had been sexually promiscuous before the public became aware of AIDs and he contracted the virus before it was diagnosable. Five-times-a-week analytic work over six years gradually enabled him to minimize his anxiety about genuine closeness. A turning point occurred when I told him he had to go to the hospital to withdraw from the valium use that he had increased when I was away on vacation in our third year of analytic work. I remember him staggering into the office, collapsing on the couch, and when I insisted that he check into a hospital immediately in order to withdraw from the valium, he sat up and sobbed saying "*You really care about me more than the money.*" He did go to the hospital and his withdrawal process was serious, probably exacerbated by the virus we knew nothing about.

In the fifth year of treatment he managed to risk involvement with a steady partner after years of promiscuous sex at the bath house, popular in the 1960s and early 1970s. Richard and Tom, his partner, moved to their upstate home where he died from complications of AIDS in Tom's arms.

Richard and I experienced exasperation, frustration, and concern for each other over the years of consistent work, and he holds a permanent place in my heart. We felt a special kind of love for each other. Not transference love—but real caritas. He saw that his mother lived *through* him, and over the years he learned that I cared *for* him.

As I review our work today, I see even more clearly that Richard's struggle, in developmental terms, hinged on his need for maternal acceptance as a separate individual, something she was unable to do. Margaret Mahler's research describing her separation-individuation theory had just been published in 1975 and had not been accepted by the psychoanalytic establishment. But I was lucky to be in a seminar with her and learned about her work.

Richard's attachment through identification with his mother deprived him of the fun that children need to help them through separation difficulties. Being with her constantly made it impossible for him to play with other kids and to find his own interests. It was as though he had to sacrifice everything at the peril of experiencing annihilation anxiety. I am not talking about his homosexuality but about his identity as a separate person.

As therapists, we cannot know what really went on in our adult patients' minds when they were children, or even what they actually felt, but we must remember that they did the best they could. This is what the therapist must remember and pass on to her patient. I have seen this understanding alleviate the shame and guilt that prevents the development of self-esteem so necessary to moving ahead in life. This is the conviction we need in order to do this work that is very different from just listening to free talk and giving interpretations. I can anticipate the arguments that patients like Richard and Jill and Anna in the masochism chapter are not analyzable or that the treatment I propose is not analysis.

My answer is that many so-called neurotics in classical analysis go from one identification to the next without ever finding their own authentic selves. The treatment I am proposing recognizes transference, reluctance, dream work, and the unconscious, within a frame, but it features the connection by honoring and engaging in conversation and self-disclosure when appropriate. I prefer explanation to interpretation, and ego-building along with defense analysis. I have seen that when individuation is accomplished, the patient is free to make sense of his symptoms. Working through entails mourning the old and welcoming the new.

Separation-individuation requires degrees of cooperation between mother and child. But, when a mother is too needy and anxious, for whatever reason, the child senses that moving away from her is dangerous. When a mother's anxiety or depression prevents her from encouraging or even permitting her child's thrust towards separating, this important developmental step is compromised. Thanks to my patients I began to see that beneath Freud's concept of oedipal castration anxiety that I was learning in class, lay intense separation anxiety that Richard had dealt with by identifying with his mom. I believe that his freedom was seriously compromised by his mother's combined adoration and desperate neediness. Her need to have him with her became his need even when he wanted to play with other kids. Instead he accompanied mother to the beauty parlor and the dressing rooms where she tried on clothes thus exposing him to her nudity. This must have been sexually arousing and would explain his constant teasing behavior with women. Seducing women into his bed and then disappointing them happened enough to make me wonder— did he want to be straight on some level? How did he wish I could fix him with that tool kit?

As I look back, I think he did wish I could fix him on some level, but he camouflaged this wish with his teasing. Gay Pride has just begun and there was not the acceptance we have today. In analysis we had the opportunity to connect his mother's seductive behavior to his own and the insight was sobering. It was an 'aha' moment without criticism and it alleviated his shame.

To make matters worse, Richard's father was uninvolved and remote. His older brother shattered Richard's idealization when he stood passively by in sixth grade watching as Richard was beaten up by bullies.

Fortunately, our work slowly helped Richard build his self-esteem which permitted him to express the anger that he had been turning on himself. As I review Richard's analysis, I wonder if a male therapist who was aware of and able to provide a nurturing yet masculine role model for Richard would have helped him more than I did. But my consistent presence was important to him, and one day he told me how much it meant: *"I guess I'm not all that bad 'cause you haven't given up on me."*

Patients who have grown up with psychotic, severely depressed, alcoholic, or pathologically narcissistic caretakers who have abused them physically or with neglect and constant criticism, usually need to protect themselves from remembering their painful childhoods. Instead, they seem doomed to repetition. Denial, identification with the aggressor, projection, and projective identification are defenses that are hard to give up. Preserving the parental object may mean an inability to differentiate self and object. The connection to a good enough object who can offer constancy without being intrusive or controlling sets development back on track.

People who have been poorly treated as children often end up replicating the past by becoming just like the original abusive object (identification with the aggressor) or by choosing objects to be with who are just like them. The reasons are complicated and multi-determined; one is the wish for a better outcome, and another is the need to hold on to the familiar abuser. Stress causes epigenetic changes, and intergenerational transmission of trauma is almost always a factor. Neuroscientists might mention the neural pathways in the brain that explain habit and the seeking of the familiar (addiction to abuse). And we mustn't overlook childhood depression. I often wonder if children who make the most noise both literally and in their rebelliousness are not only calling for help, but in fact warding off depression.

Relationships are usually sadomasochistic, and the cycle of pain continues. In therapy the patient will try to seduce the therapist into repeating the past in myriad and often subtle ways. Rather than feel or experience one's own rage, the patient often tries to project it onto the therapist. This tendency must be pointed out consistently over many years of work but never with criticism.

I don't mean all this to sound simple. It is hard work. In fact, the therapist often becomes discouraged, angry, frustrated, frightened, and sometimes either consciously or unconsciously arranges to end the treatment by breaking the frame. Leonard Shengold (1989) says in his book *Soul Murder: The Effects of Childhood Abuse and Deprivation*:

> *Those who have been subjected to attempts at soul murder require one quality from the therapist or analyst above all others: patience... To accept the analyst as a separate person and then as a predominantly benevolent one takes years of seemingly endless repetition and testing... The analyst and the patient must be able to last it out... Interpreting aggression toward the analyst in such a way that the patient can make use of it requires great skill, perseverance, and (again) patience* [pp. 311–317].

Dr. Shengold's last sentence is the key to working with severely troubled patients. Many of these patients have buried and/or split off their rage, and can function quite well in many areas, but the avoided and acted out rage takes a toll, particularly in the area of relationships. Carrying rage is like carrying a time bomb; closeness and intimacy feel dangerous and are not ordinarily risked. In order to resume development such a person must be helped to recognize, tolerate, and understand their rage in treatment. Such tolerance and understanding lead to acceptance and to the realization that rage is one of many emotions. This happens slowly and painfully through reliving the past with the analyst as both transference and new object. When rage gradually becomes object-directed anger, growth has taken place. When the patient can feel both love and hate without fearing retaliation or merger, mature relationships become possible. This is why a major childhood achievement is the development of ambivalence.

Patients need to test the therapist's ability to tolerate their rage over long periods of time. What is really being resisted is the idea of separateness. Severely troubled patients often do not want to feel differentiated from the object. In such cases the expression of anger threatens the patient with annihilation, fragmentation, loss of self, loss of the object, and loss of love. A goal is expressing anger with words. In order to trust the therapist, abused patients will test. In order to pass these tests the therapist must remain consistent, calm, firm, and consciously alert to signs of the patient's rage. Roadblocks are signals of the patient's split-off or suppressed rage and they include:

- *Missing appointments (especially with no telephone call)*
- *Forgetting to pay the bill*
- *Coming late repeatedly*
- *Expressing anger at people outside of therapy (especially on the way to therapy)*
- *Wanting to quit therapy or cut down sessions*
- *Experiencing depersonalization or even dissociation*
- *Reporting violent and sadistic dreams that are disavowed or disowned*
- *Experiences of psychosomatic pain*
- *Self-mutilation and self-injury (accident-proneness)*

Therapeutic attitudes that tell the patient that it is not safe to feel rage are:

- *Agreeing with the patient's wish to cut down or end treatment prematurely*
- *Rearranging appointments frequently at the patient's request*
- *Answering most questions without exploring them*
- *Letting the patient run up a bill or not charging for missed sessions*

- *Changing policies in general, such as extending session time*
- *Forgetting or being late for sessions*
- *Treating the patient as if she does in fact have a time bomb (tiptoeing)*

I learned, starting in my clinic days, that despite the roadblocks, the detours, the fear of change, each and every person I met wanted (deep down) a second chance to live richer, fuller, more meaningful lives. They certainly didn't admit this easily, if at all, but this wish is what allowed them to come to therapy, whether mandated or not.

Clinging to misery

Some patients hold on to the abusing object through the pain of repeated injury, ongoing stress and tension, mental anguish, and addiction. They may court physical pain by visiting doctors frequently, complaining, yet never letting them succeed in alleviating the pain. This kind of interaction expresses both the wish for closeness and the fear of it. Even pain is addictive, a fetish, a perverse attachment to an internalized abusive object. Pain has magical powers: it can assuage guilt about being separate, it can contain rage and its attendant anxiety, it can protect against unbearable loneliness because it is always available. One patient said that her pain was like a friend—always there for company. The internalized abusive object representation is threatened by treatment. Wishes for something better cause anxiety, and medication may be necessary. As patients begin to realize their accomplishments they may leave treatment abruptly, perhaps by setting up a situation that requires a move, by running out of money to pay the therapist, or by slowly provoking the therapist into ending the work.

The therapist must realize that an adult survivor of childhood abuse will never fully trust another. But just the realization that there *is* an other is a major achievement. The act of differentiating causes great pain, but this is the pain that leads to growth.

Quoting Leonard Shengold again from his book *Soul Murder (1989):*

> *"To accept the analyst as a separate person and then as a predominantly a benevolent one takes years of seemingly endless repetition and testing.... The analyst and the patient must be able to last it out."*

It takes stamina to do this work along with a profound sense of benevolent curiosity, respect, hope, and love. The rewards are sometimes difficult to see but over time, those who do this work experience their own growth alongside the patient's growth—and for some of us this means the world.

True individuation is an ongoing process in my mind, both in the representational world and in the real world. An encouraging partner is always helpful and this is what I mean by the power of connection.

Richard grew tremendously and it was a tragedy that his life was cut short before he could fully enjoy all that he had accomplished.

CHAPTER 7

RIFF: LEVELING THE PLAYING FIELD

Can We Talk?
— Joan Rivers

The analyst listens to the patient with a special kind of attention enhanced by varying years of experience, reading, and studying. She proposes the frame and preserves boundaries. But once analyst and patient agree to work together are they bound to asymmetry? Or can the dyad walk together towards the problems, with both searching for answers without a tilted relationship? I propose the term co-travelers on a journey. I see the work as requiring a partnership in search of truth.

As comrades-in-arms the dyad works for the same purpose: growth. I see us as collaborators who pool resources. Some call this the working alliance and others say everything is transference. I am suggesting a parallel effort with the shared motive of solving mysteries.

Does one walk behind or ahead of the other when conditions are stormy? Good question. I propose walking side by side. Storms affect both travelers whose partnership is both supportive and searching. Of course, storms are metaphors for emotional upheaval, and in these instances it is the guide who stands by. His presence is reassuring. He realizes that he and his partner can survive and even thrive. If they are to create something new, each partner must allow thoughts and feelings to run freely. Each may choose how and when to share what occurs to them but because of this cooperative work, both analyst and patient are bound to be authentic searchers on the journey.

What happens when there are roadblocks along the way? Sometimes the dyad walks around the impediment and sometimes the partners remove it by understanding what it means, thus allowing them to continue traveling. Regarding intense negative feelings and their opposite, the dyad figures out if they're a distraction or if they are clues. For instance are the feelings of love substituting for what was missed early in life. If so, why dismiss them? Discovering a new feeling or remembering an old positive one strengthens the travelers. When anxiety or depression impede the travel they register it, stay with it , and figure it out. Some see depression as caused by a chemical imbalance correctible by drugs. But what caused this chemical imbalance? Feelings!

The hormones Cortisol, secreted during anxiety, and Oxytocin, called the love hormone, affect mood and this is what is meant by chemical imbalances. A special kind of love grows during the journey allowing for the expression of anger. What causes anger? A narcissistic slight in which case we stay on that island until we figure it out together, and if it's something the therapist inadvertently or mistakenly said or did, an apology is in order. We don't let negativity build so much so that we exhaust ourselves by fighting. We explore the anger, putting it where it belongs. By apologizing we show the traveler something that may feel new (it has to be spontaneous and genuine.)

I once heard a case where the analyst, startled by thunder-and-lightning storm, looked out the window while the patient was talking. The patient got furious. I think I would have just said "I'm sorry, I was startled" instead of working it out during the patient's fury. Later I would have found a place to say something like: *this reminds me of the time you got upset when I was startled by the storm. It felt to you as though I'd forgotten you. As I thought about it I remembered that you were left once by someone who was distracted when you were a child and I wonder if my looking out the window reminded you of that.* The basic goal being to explore what we perceive in the service of understanding.

Regarding the couch: I hope that our institutes have freed their students from the inherited custom regarding the use of the couch. Freud felt comfortable with his patients using his divan (not the flat couch with pillow that so many use today.) But I fear that his preference has become an ingrained, fetishistic artifact. The idea of demanding or insisting that a patient use the couch is ripe for debate. Such an arrangement can be seen as putting a patient in a subordinate position to the analyst. It also may imply illness and it can be seen as infantilizing. But most of all, it can serve to avoid the connection between two people. Some patients use the couch to avoid connecting. Using a reclining, swivel chair with ottoman would allow the patient to choose looking away from or at the analyst. (For most of my career I preferred the couch but if I were to start over I would leave it up to the patient and would welcome face-to-face at least part of the time.)

While we analysts value regression, which for some people can happen more easily by using the couch, we also value improved object relating. Many patients have been stuck developmentally and I believe that the most important aim of our work is the resumption of development. With all that we have learned from neuroscience and developmental psychology, seeing another person's face and the ability to turn away is a vital aspect of development and it also respects autonomy. Remember that Freud, for reasons that are becoming clearer, avoided the early maternal bond and that he did not like being looked at all day.

CHAPTER 8

WHAT HAPPENS IN PSYCHOANALYTIC TREATMENT? WHAT'S IT ALL ABOUT

> ...each time a memory is recalled, the encoding of that memory becomes potentially changeable—i.e., the encoding process puts that memory trace into a plastic state, and can be retranscribed, before it is buried again.
>
> —Norman Doidge

What happens in psychoanalytic treatment? How is it different from behavioral type therapy? Why does it take a long time? And why is it often so hard for people to change? What is the reason for taking a journey inside? Why do some differentiate psychoanalysis and psychoanalytic psychotherapy? And why do some leave the trip before it's over? And is it ever over?

My hypothesis at this moment is: As treatment progresses, the patient gradually puts into words the envy-fueled rage, the fears of separation, the dread of dependency, the hope to be accepted, and the pain of unrequited love that she has repressed or acted out and sequestered in her fantasy world. Guilt diminishes. Closeness becomes possible. The lenses through which a person sees that have been shaped by early impressions of their reality, change and shift perception. In many instances early caretakers have been absent, abusive, intrusive, neglectful, and/or narcissistic. The manner in which these early figures and their actions are registered by the brain (internalized) depends on the child's perception and colors its future perceptions, along with its age-appropriate ability to process relationships and events that include its own drives, fantasies, hormone levels, and developing defenses. Through working with the transference, with the analyst informed by the countertransference, these experiences take on new shape and the self and object world changes. Perceptions that had been black and white and one dimensional expand into colorful multidimensionality. Lisa, towards the end of analysis, developed a sense of color and shape that she had not experienced before.

A false self fades as it becomes unburdened by the need to please. Self esteem builds as the ego strengthens and the superego loses its harshness. My view is that new experiences with the analyst, some of them emotionally corrective, change the body chemistry and stress level. Different brain pathways that exist along side of the old ones are used.

As the lenses widen and vision deepens reparations are made and the energy spent on once needed but crippling defenses is freed. The past gets revised due to fresh perception.

Respect for the early defenses as adaptive alleviate shame and as shame diminishes pride becomes comfortable. Distortions are recognized. The internalization of the analyst and of the analytic process is thought to occur when the hormone oxytocin is released by positive and even erotic transference. Here is the opportunity to stop the repetition of the past and to move on. The loving aspects of the self, originally perhaps shaded over by early trauma, become available enabling recognition of the other as different from the self. Empathy becomes possible. Anger subsides. Forgiveness is possible, and the past is mourned. The years spent in analysis has to change the brain.

I have tried to tease apart and also to integrate some theoretical understanding of what I think goes on in psychoanalytic work. Jurgen Reeder in *"Hate and Love in Psychoanalytic Institutions"* spoke of the analyst finding her own voice. I would add her own ears. I hope we all do that—and find ways to modulate them with each patient. My special thanks to Norman Doidge's book "The Brain that Changes Itself" along with his personal communications introducing me to the plasticity of the brain which to me, along with internalization of the analytic experience, accounts for new growth. To those who believe that plasticity ends at a certain age, my own experience tells me otherwise.

Psychoanalytic work is based on the observation that individuals are often unaware of many of the factors that determine their emotions and behavior. These unconscious factors can cause unhappiness, sometimes in the form of recognizable physical symptoms and at other times as troubling personality traits that cause problems in work and/or in love. By learning on an emotional and cognitive level how past difficulties have shaped the present, a person has a chance to grow beyond them. Psychoanalytic work entails degrees of re-experiencing childhood difficulties with a new object, leading to a different outcome—one that leads to the resolution of symptoms and increased happiness and productivity. But, as much as people want change, it's difficult to step out of their comfort zone as painful as it may be. Why? What we know seems safer than the unknown. What we are used to means safety. So there's the rub. I see these fears of change as roadblocks on the journey and it takes two to deal with them.

The connection between two people—in this case patient and therapist—is the most potent game changer in my opinion. These two unique individuals form a special bond as they explore and re-explore whatever occurs to them. Thoughts, feelings, dreams, wishes, fears, ideas, beliefs, opinions, are expressed both in actions and words, both consciously and unconsciously. They develop a unique rhythm, pace, trust, respect, and humor which frees them to express negative and positive feelings. They play together and hopefully stay together for as long as they like, and they end their meetings with the knowledge that their relationship has become a part of them.

Psychoanalytic treatment usually involves meeting numerous times weekly with an educated therapist and attempting to talk freely about thoughts and feelings. The frequency of sessions is important for a person who wishes to become aware of the underlying sources of his or her difficulties, not simply intellectually, but emotionally—by re-experiencing them in the treatment with the analyst. Through this process the dyad works together to solve the mysteries. An important clue is the ways the patient relates to the analyst because we all have the tendency to transfer feelings and fears from early objects on to new objects. Another clue is learning what the patient is hesitant to talk about and the reasons why.

As the work progresses patterns emerge in dreams, memories and behaviors. Making sense of all this leads to growth and the capacity to change. Through this process development that was derailed proceeds. For instance someone who hasn't adequately separated self and object or succeeded in tolerating ambivalence cannot tolerate the 'idea of the 'other.' We see this on the grammar school playground where kids who are different are excluded. I see racism similarly.

Insecurity stemming from parental and societal attitudes along with many other factors play a large role in the difficulties one encounters. The adolescent may turn inward, become depressed, construct a narcissistic bubble, become a bully or a victim, all attitudes that cause him grief due to isolation. Psychoanalytic work varies in intensity and often deepens as the partners travel. But engaging such patients takes a skill that I talk about in *Deepening the Treatment.*

Eventually the traveler reaches a point where she can travel on her own. She becomes her own guide, equipped to see life through new lenses, to navigate rough spots with new skill, and to continue life's journey with new strengths. I cannot prove this, but I believe that defenses we form early in life require psychic energy and so letting go of these once adaptive mechanisms releases the energy we need in order to move on.

Paradoxically, the real goal of psychoanalytic work is double edged for it entails the ability to connect to others and to be self sufficient. However, autonomy and connection are not like oil and water. Actually the former enhances the later. We all like to lean on someone once in awhile—but relationships that are based primarily on depending are often doomed to fail. The disappointments in a partner or even a friend can become overwhelming and can destroy connections if they are based only on need. Sure, people need each other for different things and at different times but the ability to stand on one's own two feet is what builds the self esteem we all need. Kahil Gibran wrote about this in *The Prophet* where he said:

> *"stand together, yet not too near together: For the pillars of the temple stand apart, And the oak tree and the cypress grow not in each other's shadow."*

Behavioral therapies like CBT are quite popular and work for many people with specific issues. But those who want lasting results move into psychoanalytic work.

Returning to a travel analogy, the therapist/guide is enriched by each voyage she takes. She learns more with each unique journey. Her experiences inform her every day. And although she realizes that there are some common themes, she values and respects uniqueness. Sometimes the voyages last a long time.

As the journey progresses, the client/patient tells the stories of his life. She tells them in different ways and as she travels she finds old friends and enemies, places and people she has forgotten about, events that stand out, and emotions and fantasies that have been buried or pushed aside. As she gradually puts into words the love and hatred, the envy fueled rage, the fears of separation, the dread of dependency, and the pain of unrequited love—laughter and a new appreciation of life emerge, first in the relationship with one's travel partner and then with others. Scenes shift. New light casts different shadows that reveal and even create new sights. Shame melts with the light. Guilt is diminished. Intimacy becomes possible. Needs change. Talents blossom. Symptoms disappear as strength increases. Along the way the guide or co-traveler is a substitute for past objects but the level playing field helps avoid getting stuck. *"Who me?"* the analyst said when 20 year old Sam accused him of judging his new girlfriend. *"Could it be that you're mixing me up with your dad."* This sounds corny or less than elegant but we gear our language to the particular patient quite naturally. The idea is to help Sam see and feel the difference. Sometimes we therapists, in our attempts to be neutral forget that being spontaneous and genuine works best.

The lenses through which a person sees have been shaped by early impressions of one's reality. I am saying that reality changes with growth. A one year old handed a five dollar bill might chew on it or tear it up while a twelve year old would use it quite differently. So one's sense of reality depends on experience, and the experience that can be useful depends on degrees of cognitive ability and independence, and on needs. A sixteen year old's reality is different from a three year old's reality because motor skills and cognitive comprehension are more sophisticated. Even size matters.

In many instances early caretakers have been abusive, intrusive, neglectful, and self-involved. Sometimes loss or illness or poverty has taken a toll. The manner in which these early figures and their actions are registered by the brain (internalized) depends on the child's perception at the time and this colors its future perceptions, along with its age-appropriate ability to process relationships and events. Perception is effected by states of mind, by fantasies, and by the development of defenses among many things we have yet to discover. For instance if a baby is left alone when sated as opposed to hungry, the absence of the feeder will be reacted to differently. If the baby feels hungry for hours every day as opposed to once in awhile the reaction will differ. Also, as made clear by many authors including Piaget (1929), experience is encoded differently depending on the ability to use words. The infant's experience may not have reached a level of specificity and organization required to be accessible and relatable. In cases of early abuse the analyst's ability to be with his patient empathically must take precedence. Shengold (1999) says:

> *"The therapist of the victim of soul murder (and of others not significantly traumatized or deprived as children but similarly psychologically burdened) requires the utmost in empathic tact and patience to guide the patient toward becoming able to tolerate the need for love. Love must be felt in order to acknowledge and attenuate the terrible legacy of murderous hatred that has become too much to bear without destructive or self-destructive action accompanied by crippling inhibitions and defenses. Restoring the capacity to care about oneself and others is the therapeutic challenge"* (p. 286).

Working with the transference (with the analyst informed by her own transference) allows experiences to take on new shape. We might even say that the inner self and object world of the patient gradually shifts OR we might say that new relationships are registered in the brain. Perceptions that had been black and white and one dimensional expand into colorful multidimensionality. A false self fades as it becomes unburdened by the need to please. Independence is not always realized as I have said before due to one's pull towards the safety of the familiar. So *working through* is an apt phrase because it does require two at work to pull away from what is familiar. When I first listened to certain jazz music it made no sense but as I continued to listen it grew on me.

My view is that positive new experiences with the analyst decrease stress levels and the body chemistry changes. The experience of being listened to by a non-judgmental other is usually a new one and it takes time to trust it. Both cognitive and emotional growth permit internalization of the newly perceived object thereby forming new neural pathways in the brain that exist along side of the old ones or perhaps blend with them (Doidge, 2007). As the lenses change and vision deepens reparations are made and the energy spent on once necessary but crippling defenses is freed. The past gets revised due to fresh perception.

What was experienced by the child changes when the adult looks back with new perceptive ability. For instance, size alone changes how we see. A toddler must look up at an adult. As the toddler grows, the view changes. The adolescent grows to tower over the parent in many cases. But the early view seems to form the pictures we store in the mind. (This is a simplistic idea because we can't know what a child registers—we use theories of child development in our assumptions that are based on careful observation.) How often do adults see themselves as children in the presence of their parents. Or the reverse, how often do parents see their adult offspring as children. Travelers on the psychoanalytic journey learn to adjust to changing reality. Shame diminishes and pride becomes comfortable. Distortions are recognized.

The internalization of the analyst's benign curiosity and of the analytic process is thought to occur when the hormone oxytocin is released by positive and even erotic feelings. Here is the opportunity to stop the repetition of the past and to move on. The loving aspects of the self, originally shaded over by early trauma and ongoing discomfort, become available, enabling recognition of the 'other' as less and less distorted and as separate. Empathy grows. Anger subsides. Forgiveness is possible, and the past is mourned. Sounds pretty neat? Well it isn't when you're going through it. Revisiting old sites with a reliable guide is required. Each journey is unique.

I ask the therapist to consider conversation. As it is often presented in the institute when discussing classic psychoanalysis, the patient free associates and the analyst makes interpretations. What about talking things over—what about conversing and exchanging ideas? Many patients I have worked with never had the opportunity to talk intimately with non-critical adults. Instead they talked at each other. Why is conversation not mentioned in our training programs or in our literature. Surely a big part of connecting is conversation. How else do we learn from each other?

But how do all these things really happen. First I will talk about what some analysts mean by self and object representations. The word 'object' means people and even parts of a person that we store in our minds. For instance:

Donna remembered her mother as a scary and remote stranger. After she was born her mother suffered a deep depression and was hospitalized for three months. A nanny cared for Donna for the first year. When mother took over, Donna became withdrawn and the mother-child relationship went downhill from there (Hardin, H.T. & Hardin, D.H., 2000). Mother's mood swings frightened Donna and as she grew up she felt unworthy. We might say that both self and object representations were quite negative. But, as any daughter would, Donna also wanted and needed her Mother's love. Torn by desire and rage Donna tried to win her mother over by being a good girl while at the same time pushing her mother away. They danced erratically to the music of mother's mood swings and daughter's efforts.

At first Donna's rebellion was directed at her mother but as time went on, rebelling became part of her character. The part of her that needed freedom along with her wish to be loved created conflict. Wanting to be a good girl and wanting to get rid of mother clashed and this was repeated in future relationships. Donna charmed men and as they came close she unconsciously pushed them away. During the analytic journey, Donna began to see that failures were multi-determined. Failure in school was not only a call for help but also a way to disappoint her mother imago and to punish herself. No one seemed to notice so Donna grew up battling herself.

While on the journey, she tried to sabotage all progress. She lost jobs and opportunities. Eventually the analyst became the object of her rage. Donna's goal became defeating the analyst/guide in several ways. One was not applying what she learned to her life. Another way was threatening to end the journey prematurely. The analyst was able to contain these wishes to defeat the trip and to explain what was happening so that Donna could keep going. How she did this rested on her belief that Donna deserved to see things differently. Analysts differ on how to work with the negative transference—some allow it to blossom and others interpret it more quickly. Of course it depends on the unique patient. Anger sometimes needs to be expressed safely in treatment. Other times it is used as a roadblock. The analyst chose to try stepping out of the transference. She said something like:

> *Donna, let's try to figure out what's going on with us. I can see you're angry but could there be more to the story?*
>
> *Donna: I'm just fed up—we've worked hard and I can't seem to change. Why!!!*
>
> *Analyst: Well, I can think of a few things but they would be my slant. Can you think of anything? I don't want to presume like your Mom did. In fact, one problem is you've transferred your experience with her on to me which is natural but not always helpful.*
>
> *Donna: (silent for minutes) Yeah, I know you're not her—maybe—wow, I just thought of this—maybe if I do start to succeed I'll not have to come here and I'd lose you.*

Analyst: I know what you mean cause I felt that way when I was in analysis. I eventually realized I could keep him in my head—and whenever I felt like it I could imagine having a conversation with him.

Donna and her therapist talked about the idea of remembering people who matter and how soothing these memories are.

Change is difficult and the road was bumpy but, over time, Donna noticed a difference. The main point here is that by reliving the conflict while on the journey, the traveler experiences old fears with growing comprehension and strength. She also sees that the guide hears her, stays with her, and does not criticize or abandon her. This allowed Donna to identify with and to internalize her therapist's attitude, alongside the troubling mother representation. In my mind, this new internalization which begins as identification, is the change agent in psychoanalytic work and it strengthens object constancy. All the conversations help the dyad keep going and strengthen their bond. Conversations are helpful when the negative transference goes on for too long. I just thought of Joan Rivers who used to say "Can we Talk?"

Bill was haunted by an unsteady father. Prone to alcohol abuse his father was strict, demanding, unreasonable, and absent for periods of time. Bill became his mother's ally and helper. She leaned on him and tried to control him. He felt special. But he needed to identify with his dad to bolster his masculinity. Highly intelligent and very handsome, he did well in school. He left home after college and paid his own way through law school. He went on to have a large family of his own but all of his achievements did not give him a sense of fulfillment. He became depressed as the children grew up and left home. He divorced his wife and went into debt. Nothing could lift the depression. He was reluctant to begin therapy having experienced a failed analysis in his early 30s. But at age 65 he decided to try again with a woman analyst. It was hard for him to admit defeat to a woman who at first stood for his mother. He was a proud man, justifiably so because of his achievements and it was very difficult for him to face needing someone. As he began to tell his stories he struggled. His sense of privacy protected him at first. How could he trust another analyst after being so damaged by the first one. But, gradually, he found that being listened to was important and also soothing. Even when he expressed anger and disdain for the analyst she tolerated it and he kept going. He came to grips with his once buried complicated feelings towards his parents and as he did, his treatment deepened. He gradually stopped blaming others for their weaknesses and because he experienced his analyst's empathy, he began to feel empathic too. In other words, he softened over time. His original view that softness was feminine diminished. He remembered positive and loving moments with his dad. And slowly he changed from a strict task master to an understanding man. He spent more time with his grandchildren who grew to adore him and that softened him too. He stopped running away and instead walked towards.

In my opinion, what happened with both patients is that derailed development got back on track. Donna had been stuck spinning her wheels with a mother she never bonded with and yet needed. Her internalization of the analyst as new object allowed her to continue individuating. For those who think in terms of structural theory, you might say that her ego strengthened as she let go of certain defenses.

In Bill's case the analysis gave him new perspective that lessened his disappointment in his parent imagos. The analyst's empathy, fought against at first because it was new, gradually got through to him after many conversations. At one point he broke down in tears that had been held back for many years. When he noticed that his analyst's eyes were teary his shame lessened. The soldierly facade began to melt. Bill was awed by his new vision. We might say that the caritas shared in treatment eroded his defensive narcissism that had been blocking the light he needed. Bill's disappointment fueled his anger that had deprived him of all warmth and appreciation, both of which are necessary to the creation of a genuine and generative self.

Bill's unique story told over time to an empathic and appreciative analyst whose vibes of caritas reached and touched him provided a connection strong enough to risk caring for and about others. I think the power of love/caritas is not acknowledged by many analysts.

In sum, the analytic dyad takes a journey that is often as rugged as it is pleasurable. Both parties grow and the benefits of that growth are absorbed which means continued travel even after saying goodbye.

CHAPTER 9

LISA: HOW LONG

What is past is prologue.
— William Shakespeare

I have chosen a developmental model that includes what we understand about childhood fantasy to review the following case. However, during the first years of work I listened in terms of the ego psychology and conflict theory I was learning at the institute. The work covered a span of time between about 1981 through 2005.

One major criticism of psychoanalysis is that it takes so long. I believe this criticism deserves discussion. Why indeed? My answer has to do with respect for the *unique* individual. Depth therapy serves the patient and it is she who determines how long it takes to make sense of her life.

Many years ago I was invited to speak at a psychoanalytic symposium on a panel titled "How Long"—referring to the length of analysis. That invitation made me think about Lisa with whom I had traveled for twenty-two years. I took the occasion to contact her about seven years after we had finished our journey (see below.) This is our story.

How long does analytic work take? How far does the dyad travel? This is an impossible question to answer because no two people are alike and no two dyads are alike! But I will tell you a bit about the twenty-two year journey in two parts that Lisa and I took. By the second year we were traveling three days a week which increased by the third year to five sessions a week. During our journey we experienced frustration and fascination, boredom and inspiration, caution and courage, and the special kind of love that develops along the way. Working through the effects of Lisa's early trauma and modifying her rescue fantasy and her wish to be rescued took a long time. I begin with two letters.

Dear Lisa,

It has been some time since we ended analysis and I hope you don't mind me getting in touch. If you prefer not to answer, you know that I will understand. I would love to know how you are and if the work we did has continued to be helpful to you. There is so little research in this field and we analysts rarely see the results of analytic work (except for our own). If you feel comfortable answering, e-mail is fine with me. But please do not feel it necessary to respond.

Sincerely,

Jane Hall

The answer is condensed because it contained details of life.

Jane—

I think of you so often! I was thinking of writing a letter but I never seem to get around to these things. I completed my masters—3 1/2 years of boring hell which for some reason I was determined to do. I have been on the city council and I also completed the course requirements for my city clerks license. Again, I am not sure why this sort of thing appeals to me, but one of the many things I learned in analysis was to stop second guessing these things that feel right. I have a million other things that I often tell you. I feel like analysis is another example of inertia—That bodies (or in this case minds) in motion stay in motion. Every once in a while I realize that I'm doing something and I think—OHHHHHH, that's what Mrs. Hall meant. Of course I can't remember an example of this but it is clear to me that I am still learning from my analysis every day. If I recall correctly that is what I said I wanted very early on—to be able to accept the feedback around me. It is not always pretty but I feel like I fit into the world. I never really thought that would be possible. I find the whole subject of analysis fascinating. Annie (a friend in this field) and I talk about it—how it really does change the past. Is there any way I can help? I would love to talk to you or anyone else who wants to hear me talk about myself! I still find the whole experience fascinating. I can barely remember anything we talked about but I can physically feel the difference. I am so much more peaceful and grounded and nearly every day I stop to really appreciate something beautiful or funny or absurd. It was wonderful to get your letter. I hope you are doing well. Please let me know if there's any way I could help provide information about analysis. I am so grateful for the experience.

—Lisa

In my very first meeting with Lisa , the minute she sat down and before I heard her story, I thought to myself, based strictly on intuition, 'this is one of the angriest people I've met." I have worked with many angry people, and anger is a natural part of the work—but this was different. It was a gut feeling. You see, Lisa also impressed me as a genuinely nice person in every sense and there were no overt signs of anger. A tall, attractive, and intelligent woman in her mid-twenties, Lisa exhibited gentleness, a good sense of humor, a warm smile, and natural poise (she was stopped once in a restaurant by a stranger who said she wished her son would marry someone like her). I questioned my perception of her anger by wondering if I was envious or whether she reminded me of someone else, so I filed it away as just a possibility. Today, with my knowledge of self-states I think I was picking up on Lisa's use of dissociation. Somewhere carefully hidden, was a self-state filled with rage. Back then I had no idea about self-states.

Lisa began treatment ostensibly due to a break-up with her boyfriend, and after her withdrawal from cocaine which he had supplied. As I review her story, I see that this boyfriend and his cocaine represented her mother whose food was seen as both necessary and poisonous—but I am jumping ahead. He and the cocaine had helped her ward of the dark clouds of depression and the separation anxiety that threatened when she left home. Actually, home left her. Other family members had moved on and

Mother sold the house she was calling home. Lisa felt adrift and wanted to find out who she was and where she would fit in. She had a very good job but was aware of her authority problems, as exemplified by trouble with her bosses at work. Interestingly, she held a managerial position in which she excelled. Her team loved her.

She was referred to me by her older sister's therapist who, it turned out, worked quite differently than I did. I never knew whether our differences were due to this therapist's assessment of her patient or to her philosophy of treatment but when Lisa asked me why I did not talk on the phone between sessions or exchange recipes, she understood and agreed with my rationale.

After a few months of twice-weekly contact, while talking about her family, she offhandedly mentioned that there had been five children in her family (previously she had said there were four). It emerged that her baby brother Billy, died of SIDS when he was four months old and when Lisa was twenty-six months old. Lisa and her Mother were in the front seat of the car with Billy in the back seat when he stopped breathing. She remembered her Mother frantically trying to revive the baby and then being whisked away by the neighbor for milk and cookies. Her somewhat nonchalant tone when relating these events covered over what was to become a major theme in the analysis. Although I did not consider dissociation at the time, it would account for the lack of affect in her telling of the memory that was at least partially based on what she learned later. However, recent research has determined that a two-and-a-half-year-old, give or take a few months, can remember traumatic incidents as well as other events. We can only speculate how a two-year-old registers the death of a baby but I think it safe to say that it was registered by Lisa as traumatic. I experienced the tone of her reaction as part denial and part isolation of affect at the time.[3] (By the way, I do not think theoretically while listening to a patient. I just thought it puzzling at the time.) Lisa, like any normal two-year-old, must have had mixed feelings about the arrival of a new baby. Giving up the attention one gets as the youngest in the family can't be easy. She probably saw no reason for Billy's birth and, like most two-year-olds, wished that he would disappear. However, she did say that she wanted Billy to be her partner to even things up in the family (mother had father and her older sister had her older brother to play with.)

As far as Lisa knew, the family never spoke of Billy's death, to each other or to Lisa, until she brought it up after beginning treatment. It was hard to imagine how Susan, the eldest child, and John, the second oldest, reacted. They were at school and so were not witnesses. But Susan became a nurse and John grew up to be a troubled person so we may assume that Billy's death and its repercussions affected them. It was verified that after the death, Lisa's mother withdrew emotionally for periods of time and at one point she was hospitalized to undergo ECT for depression. Lisa remembered her mother lying on the couch unresponsive to all attempts to draw her out.

---

3 A growing body of evidence suggests that the information entered into memory is often altered in various ways over time—and these alterations can reduce its accuracy and change its meaning. Such changes fall under two major headings, memory distortion, alterations in what is retained and later recalled, and memory construction, the addition of information that was not actually present.

We came to learn during the analysis that one result of Billy's death was Lisa's buried fantasy that she had magical powers, a fantasy that impacted her life. Her wish that Billy would disappear had come true. Phyllis Greenacre (1956) wrote of the very long working-through process required when reality coincides with a wished-for fantasy in childhood. Because of this imagined power, Lisa could not understand it when she didn't get her own way, so she either rebelled or shut down. I could not imagine her acting like an entitled or bratty child but as her analysis deepened, she slowly let the anger out. She would go on strike at times by lying stiffly on the couch, refusing to talk but eventually words replaced this action. After several years of work, Lisa spoke of living her life holding her breath due to her fear of killing or dying. We learned that this was a combination of her own rage and the reality of Billy's death. Could it happen to her, she wondered. Actually, when mother lost Billy, Lisa lost her mother to depression. Lisa also suffered from survivor's guilt which fed into her rescue fantasy. These conclusions came gradually over the years of her analysis. I remember making many referrals during the beginning of our work—mostly for younger male friends that Lisa felt needed help, and one was even named Bill.

Before my first month-long summer vacation of Lisa's therapy, when she was still coming twice a week, she began a relationship with Fernando. Although she realized that he was inappropriate—he was two years younger (as Billy had been) and unsophisticated—they fell passionately in love. The relationship ended several months after I returned from my vacation but it sustained Lisa while I was away. It also indicated that if I could not be there to take care of her on some level, she would create another supporting and supportive situation. Lisa was also quite mean to Fernando. She gave him money and then resented him for taking it. I believe that her attitude reflected the mixed feelings she had about Billy. Rescuing Fernando and then then emasculating him reflected her mixed feelings. It also portended certain dynamics of our relationship—taking in my food and spitting it out.

Caretaking and being cared for were vivid themes in our work, and although I never considered the treatment as specifically supportive, I know that just meeting regularly with a therapist who listens without criticism provides a sense of safety.

Lisa's younger sister, Tina, was born three years after Billy had died when she was five years old. She too was a sickly baby requiring much attention. By the time Lisa was six or seven, and from then on, she remembered mothering Tina due to her mother's bouts of depression. She saw to it that Tina had new shoes and clothes as she outgrew them, comforted her when she was upset, and helped with homework. Lisa was too busy to cultivate her own friendships. On top of all this, Lisa's Dad, who died when she was nineteen after a long illness, traveled a lot for work during Lisa's childhood. He was described as a wonderful man who supported his wife through her depressions as best he could, and Lisa had fond memories of him—but he could not be the caretaker that the children needed. In our work, we considered Lisa's disappointment in her dad and how angry she felt.

(It must be understood that Lisa's memories, based on childhood perception were not necessarily accurate. What happened was perceived by a child. But they were, nonetheless, valid for our work. We all distort memory but the distortions are what we work with.)

Tina began drinking at age fourteen and became an alcoholic. She moved out of state, eventually gave up drinking, and lived a lesbian life for ten years, after which she married a man with an auto-immune disease and had three children. Just as Lisa had mothered Tina, Tina took on the role of caretaking with her husband as his illness progressed, and with her three children. When Susan, Lisa's older sister who was a nurse, developed a terminal illness some years after her father's death, she required increasing care. Once again Lisa's mother called on her children for help. Death and illness haunted the family and Lisa's mother, for whatever reasons seemed unable to provide a safe space for her children, at least in an emotional sense.

In her transference to me, Lisa was wary for many years. But as we worked at understanding her need to keep a distance, and as I proved reliable, our relationship shifted, sporadically at first but then steadily. In the first few years, Lisa rejected anything I said, took it home and then made it her own. Poisoned food was her unconscious fear. In fact, any pleasure felt dangerous to her. After an orgasm she would throw up, after winning a man she liked she pushed him away, and any kindness shown her was spurned even though she craved love.

Gender identity, thought to solidify at around age two, was problematic. Partly in order to be a boy for her mother who was mourning the loss of Billy, and partly because she could not identify with or take in her mother or older sister, Lisa was conflicted about femininity. After about two years in treatment, I saw her transformation as she began to identify with me. She even shopped at a store in my neighborhood and enjoyed competing with me in style. Her sadistic dreams and treatment of men continued although heavily disguised.

Lisa and I had many conversations about her mother's incapacities as possibly reflecting her ambivalence about having children (they were all troubled but functioning) and we wondered about her own childhood. All of her children suffered in their unique ways from lack of nurturance. Post-partum depression was not talked about at the time but it was a definite possibility. Her mother's brother was mentally ill, and some of her siblings had died before she was born—realities that made us wonder about genetics and her mother's difficulty with nurturing. Lisa's oldest sister, Susan, grew up to be an obese gourmet cook, and John grew up facing his own emotional difficulties. His marriage ended badly when his children were in their teens, and Susan and her husband parted ways too.

Lisa went to great lengths to hide her soft, needy side, even as a child. She remembered burying frogs and withdrawing so it was difficult to tell how much she was ignored or how much she pushed mother away. Probably both but a child's mind comprehends subjectively. At age six or seven she seemed to cover or bury her anger and neediness by caring for Tina. Suffice it to say, Lisa's development was complicated.

As I write about Lisa and her family, it begins to sound like a Shakespearean tragedy. It would be easy to explain what happened in this family by thinking in terms of genetics and chemical imbalances but as analysts we now know that chemical imbalance can be caused by states of trauma due to the production of cortisol and other hormones, or their lack, that affect the brain. It took over twenty years to modify the effects of Lisa's shock and strain trauma. Kris (1956) coined this phrase in his paper: "The Recovery of Childhood Memories." One important thing we did accomplish was stopping the intergenerational transmission of trauma. I mentioned earlier that such work is like trying to stop a speeding freight train but we managed. When Lisa had her baby after ten years of treatment, she was an excellent mother with no depression. (And she did not name her son Billy.)

Being managed was a problem as Lisa felt smarter and more powerful than her bosses (her first boss, mother, was perceived as unsafe as was her older sister who in childhood had no use for her). Authority problems abounded and this played out over the years in our work and outside of treatment.

There were many periods when Lisa's simmering rage was enacted by rejecting my ideas and efforts. She seemed unable to let me in for a long time and this made me feel inconsequential and feeling quite helpless, and sometimes angry. My benevolent curiosity sometimes failed me as I got tired of being ignored but I kept the reaction to myself. I did tell Lisa that her distancing me was important to explore. Any question I asked or intervention I made was spit out, avoided, minimized, or fought although eventually addressed on her terms. Much of the time I was the dangerous yet sought after mother in the transference and at other times I stood for Susan with whom she competed. The oscillation between fearing me and wanting me all to herself was one reason for the length of this analysis. It seemed as though a suit of armor protected Lisa's grandiose self while at the same time keeping out whatever I could offer. On the other hand, her attachment to me was obvious. She was rarely late and over all the years of work, there were hardly any missed sessions.

We can imagine how Lisa's basic conflict affected others. She made good women friends for the first time in her life but at first these friendships were filled with drama. You see, Lisa had never made real friends before so over the years she gradually resumed that developmental step that had been delayed. She even went back to college towards the end of our work and went on for a Masters degree upon ending treatment. Watching her blossom offset the rejection I felt in the first years of work.

Discussion

I wondered whether Lisa's mother found refuge in depression. When not depressed, she was a political activist, lived and traveled with a male friend some years after her husband died, but eventually decided to live on her own. When her grandchildren were old enough to be somewhat independent, she would invite them to visit occasionally, but she never seemed comfortable taking care of others.

Lisa had great difficulty in giving up on her wish or need to have me all to herself. The primitive aspect of this wish took the form of cannibalistic fantasies and dreams—swallowing me like meat. Emotional hunger and food were predominant themes throughout treatment. Although Lisa was never overweight, she loved to cook and to eat. Lisa was adamant about feeding her family healthy food. But her dreams portrayed a sadistic element. One dream in particular was about flaying human female bodies that were cooked and served in a restaurant. We learned that Lisa's early oral wishes and fantasies were connected to her fear of not being fed enough and also being poisoned. The story was that she was weaned at five months because her mother felt she took to the cup so willingly. We wondered if Lisa sensed, even then, that mother was not comfortable nurturing her. On some level she blamed Mother for poisoning Billy which we connected to her need to spit out my words. Lisa's dreams were filled with variations of mother taking away her food. We learned that these oral fears and angers were exacerbated by Billy's death. How could mother have let him die, she wondered? It was discovered that Billy was a failure to thrive baby and knowing this fit with Lisa's fantasy that mother did not feed him well enough. Younger sister Tina was also a difficult baby so Lisa witnessed again, at age five, the feeding problems and took over mothering her little sister. As I write this I see how very complex and confusing her feelings must have been as a child. Lisa had to juggle her envy of the babies, her horror at their treatment, her competition with her Mother, her exhaustion in keeping Tina alive by caring for her, her need for Mother's love, her fear that Mother's food was poison, her loneliness, her depressed mother, all potentially overwhelming. Yet she had the strength of character to not only survive, but to care for others with remarkable decency.

Lisa yearned for a good mother—a mother who would feed and nurture her emotionally and exclusively. Despite spitting out the food I offered for years, she was gaining sustenance. We wondered whether she imagined that my food was poisonous. How could she trust me when her own mother had allowed Billy to die? Could she allow herself to consciously admit to her hunger? We agreed that her problem with authority stemmed from Mother's inability to feed her children properly due to perceived incompetence, hostility, or even murderous wishes. And could she give up the wish that I would be hers exclusively? In other words, would her hunger ever be sated?

For the first year and a half on the couch tears streamed down Lisa's face constantly. From the moment she lay down to the end of the session the tears flowed. There was no sobbing and Lisa talked right through them. Our efforts to understand what they meant went nowhere. Neither free associations nor dreams seemed to explain them. The tears just kept coming to the point that we eventually stopped trying to understand them. Of course we were naturally curious about the meaning of these tears that were like a waterfall, day in and day out. (I began using two analytic napkins on the couch and she brought her own Kleenex even though I provided them.) We wondered what these tears without crying sounds or sobs meant. Did they express mourning, sadness, hostility, release of tension? Did they serve as a protective moat around her to deflect closeness or criticism? Were they emblematic of a letting go as in urination? Were they a long awaited release of tension or grief, perhaps belonging to a self-state not yet available to us. Were they meant to make me feel helpless or to elicit my empathy? Perhaps all of these. Were they coming from an as yet unidentified self-state, a state without words? Eventually we learned to accept them. Eighteen months is a very long time yet despite the tears Lisa covered a lot of ground. The tears stopped suddenly one day early in the second year of the analysis. We remarked on their curious cessation and left it at that. One idea I had was that the tears were a message that she was 'poor Lisa' and not 'powerful Lisa' so that I would not injure her with expectations or observations she had not already thought of. And perhaps 'poor Lisa' had never felt permission to express her sadness with her depressed mother. So I felt it was important to accept these tears that had been held in for so long without necessarily knowing what they meant. Just as with a crying infant, we hold them without knowing why they cry unless of course they're hungry in which case the feeding usually stops the tears. I imagined that the tension caused by a sibling's death and the worry that it could happen to her or to Tina was too much for her developing brain to handle. Today I think of a very sad self-state that conflicted with the grandiose one. My countertransference was curiosity and puzzlement.

When we ended our work after twelve years of analysis that included a seven month termination phase, Lisa had married, had progressed in her field, and was the proud mother of a healthy son. We felt that our work together had been successful and that it was an appropriate time to end the analysis. Lisa was working part time, often from home so that she could be with her son.

About three years later Lisa called saying that she was feeling somewhat depressed and she began what turned out to be another ten years on the couch. Life problems such as marital discord and a dying sister were real issues. But underneath I wondered if Lisa's unconscious fantasy that she could have me all to herself was still haunting her. We had addressed this wish in our prior work but it turned out that the fantasy of power and the difficulty in letting it go was still operative.

Summing up, somewhere in her mind Lisa was plagued by the belief that both she and her mother (perhaps not fully differentiated in her representational world at the time) had caused the sudden infant death of her four month old brother Billy when she was a little over two years old. This fantasy, which emerged slowly in our analytic work, aroused mixed feelings of grandiosity, impotence, and remorse that colored her development and affected her life. Because she repeatedly set up situations that fostered her belief in her omnipotent power, it took many years of two, three, and then five times a week work to see that she could not and did not need to control people and that she could relax. Her unconscious grandiosity colored her relationships and all of her developmental phases. When she could not control the analyst, she became enraged and then depressed. She was eventually able to mourn her imagined power, which increasingly gave her room to experience her real effectiveness at work and in close relationships. She also had to work through her guilt about being a survivor. Every two-year-old wishes for the disappearance of a newborn sibling and in Lisa's case the wish came true right before her eyes. A less intense form of treatment for this intelligent, insightful woman would have proved frustrating because intellectual awareness alone would not have helped. She had to come to terms with and then to mourn her imagined omnipotence. Childhood fantasies die hard if ever, but with work they can lose their power.

Our relationship was very complicated, and I find the usual transference-countertransference thinking helpful but somehow inadequate. What seems to resonate more is the idea of me as container, and as a new object doling out food very slowly while holding a kicking, screaming infant who was also loving and lovable. It was, looking back, as if Lisa nibbled at me for all those years eventually internalizing me as a safe mother whose food was not poisonous. The analytic process was nurturing but there was a sadomasochistic enactment going on for many years. My doodling during sessions illustrated my frustration. But I was convinced that beneath the tears and words something good was happening. Our connection grew but it was hard-won, and it fluctuated at first. It was as though Lisa was growing up while already an adult. But that's what the journey is about—growing into and then owning one's adult self. I worried about the length of the analysis. Many analysts stand ready to criticize such long-term work. And of course, I genuinely liked her and the income so I consulted colleagues from time to time. Her anger, which had been building underground, was enacted for a long time in therapy before she verbalized it. I wonder to this day if witnessing a sibling's death at such a young age is actually more terrorizing than I can ever really know. And it makes me question whether anyone can truly know another's pain and fear.

During Lisa's treatment I was thinking in terms of ego defense. It seemed to me that reaction-formation, among other defenses, was operative due to her kindness and concern with others. Lisa's personality served to hide her sadistic side that showed up in dreams where she devoured human flesh, and in treatment as she spat out my contributions for years. Today I see that Bromberg's theory of dissociation explains Lisa far better than the concept of ego defenses and the structural theory I had learned at the institute.

I mention this because although I do not consciously think in terms of theory, I see how it might have helped me better understand my countertransference.

I also wonder how Lacanians, or Kohutians, or Bionians would have worked with Lisa. But I do sincerely believe that just being there and building our connection, while explaining what I could, musing together, meandering as we did, allowed Lisa to resume development in a healthy way—without the pressure of warding off death.

Hanging in there, trying to understand, tolerating Lisa's perceptions of me while also pointing out her belligerence and her murderous rage kept us working. The fruitful periods in our work increased despite the anger she finally expressed, and we both knew that our connection was secure despite the rage.

Through it all I knew that there was what I call a special kind of love—like the *caritas* Shengold spoke about. At first a scary, desperate love—both guarded against and treasured—and then, gradually, a more trusting love on both our parts. Lisa saw that she could not kill me and that I would not kill her. It is quite amazing how well put together people can seem when carrying such heavy burdens.

It has been established that the brain is plastic, and I witnessed what might be corroborating evidence. One day, late in treatment, Lisa was redecorating her living room and came in talking about experiencing a new sense of color—and a new spatial understanding. She was delighted and surprised. A lifting of depression might explain this but I like to think that her brain rediscovered or even developed new abilities, new neural pathways as described in Doidge's *The Brain That Changes Itself*, mentioned throughout this book.

This twenty-two year analysis, conducted five times a week with a break after the first twelve years, was life-changing. The frequency helped us both withstand the hostile and fearful transference/countertransference, and to tolerate the intimacy that had seemed so dangerous to Lisa. Seeing each other almost every day for all those years allowed Lisa to realize that neither of us were murderers and that she could be a good mother and wife. Of course, I grew too.

As she mourned Billy, her father, her fantasized omnipotence, and the end of our work, Lisa grew to enjoy her new maturity. She learned about her omnipotent fantasy and conquered it to a large degree (she went into politics for several years, where she was very effective using her energy productively). She learned that closeness and the ability to depend did not mean danger or death. She truly blossomed, and I am grateful and proud to have been a good enough guide.

As stated, I was concerned about the length of this work and some colleagues criticized it at a meeting on impasse. I learned then that no one can really know better than the dyad what is best. It reminded me that the patient establishes the pace, not the analyst. I have focused on the oral meanings of this work, but over the years we covered so much more: Lisa's sexual identity, certain procrastination issues, and of course her hatred and fear of authority, to name a few. And when we embarked on our second journey, we were able to deepen and solidify our understanding.

Working with Lisa helped me re-mourn my own losses, and I'm sure that I internalized some of her qualities.

CHAPTER 10

RIFF ON LISTENING USING JAZZ

The most important thing I look for in a musician is whether he knows how to listen.
— Duke Ellington

The dyadic expansion of consciousness model conceptualizes growth, in normal development as well as in psychotherapy, as occurring when two individuals interact in a way that results in the disorganization of old meanings and the emergence of new meaning.
— E.Z. Tronick

It is only in playing that the individual child or adult is able to be creative and to use the whole personality, and it is only in being creative that the individual discovers the self.
— Donald W. Winnicott

In this chapter, because I am using jazz music to illustrate psychoanalytic conversation, I invite the reader to use YouTube on the computer. Please copy the links and paste them into your browser for an exercise in listening.

Jazz music is about making something familiar into something new. And about making something shared—a chord structure that everyone knows—into something personally unique through improvisation.

Psychoanalysts often appreciate and enjoy jazz. A few are even professional jazz musicians, and many have written about it. Why? Because the psychoanalyst and the jazz musician have something in common: the magic and spontaneity of improvisational interaction that leads to something new. I use the word magic because of the effect on both player and listener but, in actuality, beneath the improvisations is an incredibly sophisticated, complex knowledge beyond verbal explanation and often beneath awareness. We know so much that we are unaware of. Jazz improvisation uses an implicit musical structure of chord progression and melody, deeply imbedded in the musician's mind/brain/soul that he uses in his improvisations. The analyst, within her frame, uses knowledge gained from ongoing study and from experience. Both derive inspiration from their partners and from the act of creating.

I imagine that because of many variables, including genetic creative capability (talent,) memory, experience, exposure, practice, and a kind of genius, people like Charlie Parker, Dizzy Gillespie, Kenny Clarke, and others had, they were able to change the entire direction of jazz after the second world war, much in the way that certain analysts have advanced this field (see David Lichtenstein's 1993 paper using John Coltrane). The same holds true with the analyst who continues to expand on Freud's original creation.

In jazz music, with or even without chord structure (free jazz), something original is created on the spot, as in this instantly created free piece: **https://youtu.be/UtXhwUVxCjY** (Hall and Metheny.)

In solo playing, the musician is still working off internal rhythms, chords, colors, melodies, experience, mood, and the audience or imagined audience which includes the self. Players in duos, trios, quartets, quintets, all the way to big bands, free associate to and with each other by relying on their spirit, camaraderie, love, energy, openness, and wish to brave the unknown. Mistakes, lapses, even trepidations are used to further the music. References are made to old songs during many improvisations just as in the analytic literature previous texts are cited.

A force that both pulls the listener in and keeps him out, not unlike what goes on in the analytic dyad, is part of the experience. Barriers are crossed in both forms. Trust makes this possible. And if all is going well, jazz players talk about "being in the zone" or just standing aside and letting the music come out of or through them: Jimmy Raney discusses this unconscious process (**https://youtu.be/f29a1RL2lyo**)—reminding me of the reverie for the analyst and free associations for the analysand. But my focus here is on interaction because I believe it's the fuel that keeps the analytic dyad going. Here, on YouTube, is an example of traditional analytic work that seems stiff and without feeling but does illustrate free talk: **https://youtu.be/oS_L8efaJ-E**. And here's a dialogue/conversation that feels authentic **https://youtu.be/tQZPd7e8lXw.**

In this chapter on listening inspired by connection, I use the similarities between jazz and psychoanalytic work. Both aim for change. I invite the reader to listen to the selections mentioned at the URLs cited in order to experience the myriad ways of communication that cannot be expressed in words, and hope that as you listen (not all in one sitting, necessarily), your ears will grow and you will be moved. I liken the improvisations and interactions by the musicians to the analytic dyads' free talk and expressive behavior, both leading to new understanding. The point of improvising is to create something new and so jazz and analytic work share a common goal. The very essence and impression of one person on the other is what I'm talking about. It includes perception and experience. And when two people share their experiences within a structure that allows freedom, something unique happens. We are so used to searching for clues from the past that we may minimize the fact that new relationships further development. Reacting to and with the analyst's perspective or even just her presence, either consciously or more often unconsciously, changes the way one perceives, just as the jazz player is influenced by his partners. You can hear Paul Desmond in *All the Things You Are* **https://youtu.be/LDjTc8GzstQ** extend an idea he heard in Gerry Mulligan's solo and vice versa—both creating something new. This is most evident when they 'trade fours' (each play four measures to which the partner responds.) In this example trading begins at 4:16 and even before that they play together. Their attunement to each other is remarkable.

If we think about sessions as conversations, both musical and verbal, and we hear how ideas are exchanged creatively, this might help both parties in the psychoanalytic dyad understand more acutely what goes on in their work. Analysts are trained to cultivate their silence for it is felt that this allows the patient space to talk freely. And it does, but not always, and not with everyone. Similarly, the different movements in a classical piece provide periods of working through as happens in analytic work. And in our work, some patients at certain times inspire and require more interaction than at other times.

Usually towards the beginning of psychoanalytic work many patients, in my experience, find it difficult to just say what comes to mind without editing when directed or invited to do so. Some overcome the difficulty and others don't. After all, it is not a usual form of discourse, unlike jazz which relies on and is built on interaction such as call and response, or question and answer, or putting an individual spin on a piece of music. So, because connection is what we all strive for in both fields, different techniques are helpful. In fact, this is the creative part of our work—finding ways to connect. Even competition involves connection and even in silence there is connection. In both genres we lean on, break free from, ignore, embrace, argue, attack, agree, and so much more.

Freud's insistence (1912, *The Dynamics of Transference*) on what he termed *the fundamental rule of free association* became the hallmark of psychoanalysis. We tend as analysts to adhere to the rule because it is a path to discovering both how we think and what we hide from. It shows certain connections of thought that can explain the roots of symptoms but as the scope of patients widened, and perhaps even before that, free association, when imposed as *the* fundamental rule, did not take into account the unique individual and the trust required.

Throughout this book, I try to remember and to remind others that one size does not fit all. When constructing theories, we tend to forget that. Imposing rules can be reassuring but with some patients these rules deserve explanation. Paying for missed sessions can be explained if necessary. Regular appointment times often require explanation. Once a patient understands the analyst's ways of working, they are free to accept or reject them. But these frame issues are meant as safeguards that allow us to move forward. Inviting a patient to say whatever occurs to her without judging her words is far different than ruling that she do so. Don't get me wrong though. The ability to talk freely to a non-judgmental professional is helpful and even necessary to solving mysteries. In fact it is unique. Where else can one talk endlessly with the attentive listener who follows patterns and shares her ideas in the service of solving puzzles. Even the thoughts left unsaid or censored by patients can be used by them to realize why they hold back. The unspoken holds an important key. In my experience, people who come with a problem will usually say whatever occurs to them quite naturally if given the space and encouragement. However, I suspect that many analysts, while claiming to honor the fundamental rule, do not insist on it or even abide by it in their own analyses. I have spoken elsewhere about why I decry what we call a "training analysis" because I seriously wonder how much is censored. Many students avoid the negative transference and choose instead to please the analyst who is usually a member of the analysand's society.

Now, when a patient is acting out her feelings instead of verbalizing them, the partner is bound to point this out. *"The way you shut me out by rejecting everything I offer must mean something."* If this is not attended to, the analyst might become frustrated by being ignored. This is where our genuineness must take over. *"Ann, you reject my ideas all the time, yet you keep coming. I think you are telling us something important. Can we figure this out?"* With another patient we might wait. Constant disregard of the analyst/partner stalls the journey. And sometimes, unconsciously, the analyst retaliates by allowing the behavior to persist—as an expression of his anger. In a jazz quartet, the bass player is expected to keep the "time" going, and sometimes he rushes or lags behind. The leader of the group has various ways of facing the situation—from telling the player to firing him. But it must be addressed for the sake of moving forward. Whereas the psychoanalytic model offers perhaps the best insight into the private world of the individual, the dyadic-expansion model proposed by Ed Tronick offers an additional way of understanding how the private worlds of patient and analyst interact to create change. His observations on how infant and mother communicate are relevant. His research with Gold (2020) explains how the everyday mismatches or what he calls *messiness and repair* go into connection. This holds true in analysis and in jazz. Even Fred Astaire and Gene Kelly stepped on toes at times.

Alongside the analyst's listening skill is the ability to relate to the analysand with respect. As I mentioned in chapter one, I see the dyad as a partnership meant to solve mysteries using interaction. Interaction, whether transferential or based on perceived reality is, in my experience, the most important part of our work. The intersubjective school gained popularity in the 80s, and the analytic process changed for many analysts. In fact, many are now comfortable referring to analysis as a long conversation. The silent analyst has turned out to be not-so-silent after all. Yes, being quiet is valuable when used with sensitivity, however, when a patient cannot use the "fundamental rule," what do we do?

Mr. X came to see an analyst I once supervised with a problem. He could not be faithful to his wife. He loved her and was satisfied by her in all the ways he could think of, yet he kept on seducing other women successfully. After some years of psychoanalytic work, he identified the danger factor as one motive. He liked the adrenaline rush. He saw that danger was comfortable because it was familiar. Over time, he traced it back to a childhood that alternated between danger and safety. He grew up in a home where it felt dangerous to relax because of a critical and volatile father who, for no apparent reason, would often erupt with rage. This dad was also loving, and attentive but out of the clear blue sky he could change. This information did not come right away and, in fact, the analysis almost did not begin.

For some mysterious reason, Mr. X, after stating his problem in the first session, became tongue-tied. He had agreed to do analytic work eagerly after presenting the problem but when asked to talk about it or anything else that came to mind he froze. His analyst was stumped. As supervisor I was stumped too. I suggested he wait it out but nothing happened. Four times a week, X lay on the couch unable to speak. Weeks went by. In fact, he was just as perplexed as his analyst who eventually wondered if using the chair would help. X tried it but after a few sessions he began to cancel sessions and even spoke about giving up.

One day, the analyst, quite spontaneously began to talk. He said: "Well, *let me tell you what comes to my mind.*" He proceeded to tell his patient about an experience he had in a high school play when he forgot his lines. It was called *The Moonstone*—a mystery—and the audience was packed. *"My parents and girl friend were in the front row, and I was mortified when, despite prompting, I became speechless. Years later in my analysis I finally figured out that my sudden stage fright had to do with an unconscious wish to displease the director who had been flirting with my girlfriend and whom I wanted to punish by ruining the play."*

The analyst stopped to get a glass of water and when he returned X was smiling. *"It felt good to hear that story—it makes you seem human. I have been picturing you as a stiff guy who was kind of a know-it-all but your story made me see you as human. My boss is an uptight guy and you resemble him, and since I'm afraid of this boss's criticism, I felt the same about you, which is probably why I froze."*

I won't drag this story out for, of course, there is a lot more to it but I wanted to share what happened with my student because sometimes we psychoanalytic workers have to break the ice. The way we do that must be natural and spontaneous because this is what reaches and impresses the patient. Now with Mr X, the analyst had tried interpreting the silence as transference (which it obviously was) but that idea fell on deaf ears. And, of course, there was more to X's initial reaction to be discovered, but sometimes we forget the rules and go with our gut instincts. We analysts free-associate too. Jazz musicians bend melodies and use chord substitutions all the time and so do we.

Our duty as psychoanalytic workers is to learn, and to keep learning, not only about our patients but also how each interaction creates something new together. My course work experience at the institute was not helpful in this area. Fortunately, my supervisor, Martin Nass, taught me that the patient creates the theory, and I am forever indebted to him. Post graduate seminars with Gertrude Blanck, Martin Bergmann, Roy Schaefer, Jack Arlow, David Milrod, and others inspired group discussion providing a place to explore our own ideas in reaction to the literature of the time. And of course, practice is what teaches us the most. The more the musician and the therapist practice, the more they learn and grow. Remember the joke about the absent-minded maestro who was racing up New York's Seventh Avenue to a rehearsal, when a stranger stopped him. "Pardon me," he said, "can you tell me how to get to Carnegie Hall?"

"Yes," answered the maestro breathlessly. "Practice!"

Jazz musicians play. Out of that play come new ideas. The same holds true for the analytic dyad where even repetitive play can lead to object constancy.

Like jazz musicians, when the analytic dyad relaxes and feels free to say whatever occurs to them, they are playing. Both respond with what they feel inspired to contribute. Something new happens. Cliches are like transitional objects—and can be laid aside when the players feel secure and safe.

I have chosen my favorite song *All the Things You Are* by Jerome Kern, and a few other compositions to represent analytic sessions.

My hope is to inspire your listening capacity by using music. First, I direct you to explanations or deconstructions of the song by two very different musician composers:

Steven Sondheim: **https://youtu.be/VpYWY8UNA7M**

Jim Hall: **https://youtu.be/R8XUWnR8lTY**

The former is more concerned with the chord structure, the other with the melody. Personally I'm a melodist at heart because for me it implies the harmony (chords) just like the manifest content can imply what is beneath it. But we are all unique and some prefer chord structure, just as in our work we sometimes use theory to inform our listening. Actually, we hope our theories become metabolized so that we don't consciously think of them, just as jazz musicians learn the chord changes so well that they don't think of them. A simplistic example is how we read. We don't think of each letter in a word or even each word in a sentence.

John Coltrane was one highly influential saxophonist, quite opposite from Charlie Parker, an equally eminent player. Today those who prefer Coltrane are in the majority. It is easier to play off the chords than to create melody, and it's a great way to show facility. It is also easier in psychoanalytic work to ground our ideas in theory in the beginning. Listen to Coltrane playing *Summertime:* (**https://youtu.be/NEftw9o1joo**), and then listen to Parker playing the same song melodically (**https://youtu.be/j1bWqViY5F4**).

I always appreciated his approach because he takes you by the hand, never letting you feel lost—like a good a working dyad on the analytic journey.

Both state the theme but—listen and you will hear their unique approaches. And here is Charlie Parker playing *Bird of Paradise* which is his interpretation of *All the Things You Are*. He composes his own melody on the same chords illustrating how one person can explain the same story so differently: **https://youtu.be/3r4hs-yL6Zw**

Many Be-bop musicians did this for various reasons. Cherokee is another example. Charlie Parker used this song for the basis of his 1945 composition "Ko-Ko" while playing "Cherokee" (**https://youtu.be/5Ldi9sOXoBw**). He said: "I found that by using the higher intervals of a chord as a melody line and backing them with appropriately related changes, I could play the thing I'd been hearing." He had played that piece so many times that by the end he hated it, but he had mastered the chords perfectly in all 12 keys. "Ko-Ko" (See **https://youtu.be/BtYPmH1_j2A**) has a partially improvised head, and the chords are based on "Cherokee." If you don't like Be-bop, you might at least understand how and why it was created (see: **https://youtu.be/10HGVN6Qapw).** I think this speaks to identity, diversity, and mostly to creativity—which is what can bring us together. I sure hope we don't let jazz die. If you want to smile, watch these guys enjoy each other: **https://youtu.be/5Fppp8YJ8oI.**

Now, I invite you to listen to some selections featuring duets—think of analyst and analysand—with the following questions to ponder:

- *Which player is the patient and which the analyst? Do they contribute to the other's ideas? Do they even switch roles?*
- *What does the mood created convey? Does it change?*
- *What might be the content of a rendition if it used words instead of notes? The problem is usually stated first. What might they be talking about? (use your imagination freely—have fun with this exercise)*
- *What type of transference/countertransference might be occurring? What emotions are evident? Are they competing or inspiring each other? Or both!*
- *Is respect for the other operating? Or are they talking past each other?*
- *How does the session grow into something new? Is there resolution? Do you hear the question-answer dialogue?*
- *Do you hear humor or mistakes leading somewhere?*

https://youtu.be/LDjTc8GzstQ Paul Desmond and Gerry Mulligan

https://youtu.be/MsZZkOgtMyI Art Tatum and Ben Webster

https://youtu.be/WfM9bMg1NuA Hank Garland and Gary Burton

https://youtu.be/Gr_J_m1MiS8 Thelonius Monk and Charlie Rouse.

Here's a solo rendition by Bill Evans that is pure free association:

https://youtu.be/V9uZwxBkQDU

Notice he uses Parker's introduction. What do the dynamics convey to you? Loud to soft, fast to slow, playful, can you hear him surprise himself? Can you imagine his left hand as analyst and right hand as analysand? Here is a transcription for those who read music (**https://youtu.be/V9uZwxBkQDU**) And here is Michel Petrucianni with his Dad on guitar. (**https://youtu.be/wcyyLQN4gtw**), and a transcription: (**https://youtu.be/wcyyLQN4gtw**): Father and son together play circles around the song, both supporting each other and shining on their own.

What a contrast! I knew both these musicians, Bill and Michel, quite well, and their renditions capture aspects of their personalities. But what are your ideas? What are they expressing? I am not suggesting wild analysis—just encouraging you to listen and imagine. Is the theme being hidden or expanded or both? What we call resistance (I prefer roadblocks) in analytic work can also create something new. Can you hear a patient refuse to acknowledge something by saying "no, it's not that, it's this" and "this" can be a new idea as well as hiding an old idea. Also, there is an overall resistance to change that is present in all our work because what is familiar is safe. I see the interaction in jazz as particularly helpful in braving new ways of experiencing. Jazz musicians say to each other: here's an idea and the next soloist uses it to go even further.

Now, listen to and watch Oscar Peterson and Count Basie who, in this selection of *Jumpin at the Woodside,* clearly respect each other. Is Oscar inspiring Basie's awe? (see **https://youtu.be/XIs1vcoPQbw)** or is Oscar bowing to Bill Basie who made the song famous? Both idealization and a bit of competition shine through in my opinion. For those who don't know, Basie was a band leader, and Oscar was a virtuoso pianist.

If you don't like jazz, a good exercise would be listening to the Beethoven late quartets. This one was composed when he was almost completely deaf, and we can wonder what he was saying. Hearing the music played is not the same as how he heard it in his head (**https://youtu.be/XAgdd2VqLVc**).

An incredible and, in my mind, a unique connection in concerto form is in Rachmaninoff's Piano Concerto Number 2 in C minor **https://youtu.be/kS8hk0kL2sE** which illustrates the relationship between the piano and orchestra like no other concerto I have ever heard. (I admit to not having heard all, and remember I am a melodist and a romantic.) Concertos are meant to showcase the guest virtuoso. Here however, the composer gave both soloist and orchestra equally gorgeous melodies and they spoke *with* and never *at* each other. Can you hear their respect, playfulness, cooperation, and passion. The melodies are among the most beautiful in classical music and such melodies, like precious gems, are enhanced and embellished by their settings. Sometimes the orchestra plays the breathtaking melody and the piano accompanies. Then the opposite surprises us like a conversation so filled with passion, gentleness, excitement, and *espièglerie.* In the *adagio* movement, we hear such delicate support that the tenderness is overwhelming—a perfect blend of respect and *caritas* for each other. In the final movement the orchestra is given the "full moon" melody first, and sets up the piano quite elegantly—much as an analyst might say something to encourage the patient to move ahead. But then they play together, taking turns. Working through again, as we do in the last phases of our work. And finally, they feel secure enough to let an intensity take over—almost saying OK, this is really how much we feel, with no holds barred. And again, the theme is stated by the orchestra first (analyst or analysand) and both speak from the heart, neither taking over, both supporting each other. What collaboration! They become playful again, perhaps rejoicing for their success, each shining and gentle at the same time. Could there be more to say? Always! And together they give it their all—their certainty—their celebration of everything that led up to the confidence and authenticity and truth of their amazing journey. I think what impresses me most, besides the melodies, is the interaction between soloist and orchestra often playing to accompany each other and also playing together.

One more point: It is not often thought about but can you imagine the amount of work that is put into such composing. It is mind blowing as you follow the written score. Is it not comparable to the intricate life stories we hear from those who choose to work with us?

Returning to technique, a musician can play a piece in different keys—but that is technical and can lack meaning. Analysts, hearing a patient by using different theories, can experience what seems to fit, but if one learns to value intuition enriched by education, whatever occurs will be more authentic. On the other hand, and there is always at least one other hand, the ability to transpose or to change keys applies to moods and tones in an analytic session. In music I like modulations (switching keys) and in analysis we do this regularly. If psychoanalysis is anything, it is not systematic, and to expect students to think systematically takes away the nuances and subtleties in communication. In fact, getting stuck in theory is a form of binary or black and white thinking, and it is exactly this thinking that is dangerous to our work. No one is ever all one way. We have many shadings, many self-states, many ideas that may conflict more than we often know. By exploring all sides of a conflict with open minds promotes development. We draw on many strengths and propensities. And through benevolently curious conversation, we go places never thought about before. Compromise is just one solution. Going beyond gives us more strength, and this diminishes our anxieties and inhibitions when they are unnecessary.

When I graduated from the institute it took many years to unlearn much of what I was taught. Using theory can become a useful crutch especially in times of the anxiety that is natural when beginning—but it can also become a habit that deprives clinicians of their innate talents which are the true compass. Speaking of the beginning, during my first internship, while in social work school, I knew nothing. My first patient was an ex-heroin-user who I talk about in Chapter 1. Mr S did not want to be in therapy at my clinic, and I had no idea what to do. What happened is one of the best experiences I've had in all my years of doing this work. It had nothing to do with theory—it was based on common sense, courtesy, and the knowledge that connection is life-saving.

So sure, we can all recite a moment in our work where we call upon theory as a reassurance that we are doing the correct thing, but this is exactly what we must avoid. "Correct" has no place in our lexicon. Encouraging students to think this way takes them away from listening with their own ears—which become more sophisticated with experience. You see, the analyst becomes aware of her unconscious when doing her work—beyond what she uncovered or discovered in her own analyses. (Notice that I use the plural because more than one analysis is not unusual.) Each dyad naturally does this and, because each dyad is unique, the analyst never stops growing. The creative process that goes on in an analysis can never be fully explained, nor should it be. Some authors try to explain what happens in a session but the words used, no matter how well prepared or even recorded, can never tell the real or full story because of what goes on unconsciously. I used to get annoyed by authors like Heinz Hartmann who never, ever used clinical examples, until one day, I understood why. There isn't and shouldn't be a way to capture a session—even verbatim—because we miss the essence and we miss the unconscious communication going on. This is why I have chosen musical examples in this chapter. Along these lines, we must learn to trust that our patients will let us know, sometimes subtly, sometimes not, when we have erred. And we *will* err. In fact, erring is to be expected in any dialogue. But even mistakes lead somewhere. My husband, a jazz guitarist and composer, always said that a mistake (a note he was aiming for but missed) led him to a whole new place. I had the privilege of witnessing him compose a piece commissioned by the Baltimore Symphony, and only then did I realized what painstaking work was involved. I also listened to him perform solo at the White House for Duke Ellington on his birthday, and though I didn't catch it, he played a wrong chord in *In A Sentimental Mood,* written by Duke. Jim had played that song millions of times but I think Duke's presence (or maybe Henry Kissinger's had an effect. We analysts, when seeing a famous patient, react in different ways too, so it only goes to show that we're all human and can recover quite well. Our reactions to fame is a whole other topic.

Hopefully, what an analyst perceives is a unique individual who is as complex as she is. Hopefully, because we are human and often share a culture, we can empathically understand some of the fears our patients experience. Hopefully, our interaction with the patient allows us to engage in creating new ways of relating and new ideas. Hopefully, the connection we make and the explanations we come up with together and on our own, provide the strength to broaden our vision thereby changing our perception. The connection based on growing trust is a powerful force leading to growth.

Feeling angry is also a form of connection, and even murderous wishes lead to something new when understood. Occasionally, when we feel stuck, we may wonder what Winnicott, Bion, Lacan, Klein, or Freud himself would say—but *why* we feel stuck should, in my mind, be the major focus.

The medical influence (diagnosis, prognosis, cure) on this profession has shifted the essential character of psychoanalytic work: that of exploration and the effort to understand. Any attempt to force the analytic dyad into a theory or to predict an outcome can cut off possibilities. And the match counts. We each work best with certain patients based on the unconscious and conscious cues that are exchanged. This is why I dislike the concept of analyzability for it is one of those overarching concepts that does not take into account the match. It is quite instructive to listen to a group of analysts discuss a case. Educated similarly, they each bring a different point of view, just as each jazz musician interprets a piece differently, as I have tried to illustrate. Beyond the basic listening and reflective stance of analysts whose benevolent curiosity guides them, along with the guarantee against boundary-crossing, the focus is on listening and relating—not on measuring, categorizing, or curing. Psychoanalytic thinking is not like accounting or law. It is more like traveling. Only when it is over (and it is never over, in my opinion) can one try to know what happened. The idea that analytic work is "over" is a puzzlement to me. Why? Because it is a way of thinking that becomes part of us—always on hand to figure something out.

Jazz musicians are always inspired by other jazz musicians. For instance, Lester Young, John Coltrane, Charlie Parker (like some of the major theorists in this field) had acolytes or followers but the ones who find their own voices are most successful. All jazz guitarists revered Charlie Christian but those who went on to develop their own styles stood out. Most, however, stayed with that style which poses another question about growth. Barney Kessel, a brilliant guitarist who played with the best, never really changed. He found a style that worked and he kept it. Many of us do that but I hope as analysts we are more like explorers whose curiosity keeps us finding methods of travel to new destinations. Picasso kept exploring, and Miles Davis was never satisfied with what he achieved. Both were pioneers. People are said to have a cohesive self but not that long ago Phillip Bromberg elaborated on the idea of self-states. If you think about it, are you the same self when attending a funeral as you are when at a party? The phrase "out of character" loses meaning if you accept self-states—and I can almost guarantee you that if you listen to one of the music selections today, it will sound different tomorrow—you will hear different things.

My surprise in working on this chapter, which I did for a long time because I kept listening to music, is that with each draft I grew. My respect and admiration for the mind changed from fascination to awe. (Again, I suggest David Eagleman's TED Talk.) We are filled with knowledge gained from our experiences, not necessarily formal education, although that never hurts. But our registration, both consciously and out of our awareness, of what goes on around each of us and what we learn from interacting with others, is what makes us unique. Then, what we do with all those impressions can create space for new perceptions and experiences.

In sum, if we listen to and play with each other over time, we hear all kinds of utterances, moods, styles, contradictions, emotions, rigidities that shift, all making prediction dangerous. It is the surprises in analytic work and in music that have kept me going—and I wish the same for you.

Bonus: **https://youtu.be/OAVZuSoP8dk**

CHAPTER 11

STORYTELLING

Let us simmer over our incalculable cauldron, our enthralling confusion, our hotchpotch of impulses, our perpetual miracle - for the soul throws up wonders every second. Movement and change are the essence of our being; rigidity is death; conformity is death; let us say what comes into our heads, repeat ourselves, contradict ourselves, fling out the wildest nonsense, and follow the most fantastic fancies without caring what the world does or thinks or says. For nothing matters except life.

— Virginia Woolf

If you don't tell your story, your story will tell you.

— George Grosz

A colleague told me the following story about Dr. Elvin Semrad[4] who was a dynamic teacher and psychiatrist at the

4 Dr Elvin Semrad was a much-loved psychiatrist and psychotherapy supervisor who had a profound influence on hundreds of psychotherapists and psychoanalysts in the Boston area. One of his unique qualities was his ability to connect empathically with even the most psychotic patients. https://www.bostonmagazine.com/health/2014/01/28/elvin-semrad-psychotherapy

Massachusetts Mental Health Center. Many of his students became prominent psychoanalysts.

> *"On the first day Dr. Semrad gathered all 22 of us residents in his office. We had been to our wards, and knew that we were going to taking care of 50 of what were certainly the craziest people I had ever seen. Dr. Semrad smiled his Buddha-like smile and said, "Well I guess you're all wondering what articles you should be reading to help you in this work. The answer is none. If you want to know what this is all about, go find the sickest person on the ward and sit with him or her for as long as you can stand it." Dr. Semrad went on, "What you have to understand is that what seem to be bizarre symptoms to you do not seem at all bizarre to them. In fact they have evolved these symptoms as a way of coping with impossible family situations. These symptoms represent a creative adaptive endeavor. They are a work of art as much as any other work of art. Your job, and your only job, is to appreciate all these wonderful stories you are going to be hearing."*

Story telling is what psychoanalytic work is about. The psychoanalyst listens to stories, and as they are told, both parties in the dyad associate to them, and a bond is formed. This is what I see as a conversational approach with silence often as meaningful as words. As the stories become more textured they change from the first telling. Some therapists even share their own stories. However, whether the analyst's own stories are verbalized or not, they are surely evoked as he listens, helping him understand his patient. Sometimes the voyages last a long time.

The storytelling aspect of psychoanalytic work has been addressed sporadically in the professional literature. Roy Schafer's (1994) book, *Retelling a Life*, and Robert Lindner's (1982) the *50 Minute Hour* are examples. A book by Richard and Barbara Almond (1996) *The Therapeutic Narrative* uses nine classic novels to illustrate how change comes about through an interactive process. The authors compare this process to what happens in psychoanalytic work.

A favorite is *Nine Lives* by the late Newell Fisher (2019) which is required reading in all of the classes that I teach. In it he discusses nine fascinating cases in a way that I find both informative and inspiring. His style is straightforward, sensitive, and it portrays this analyst's humanity, his humility, and illustrates his love for this work. Stephen Grosz (2013) in *The Examined Life* tells the reader in short form how psychoanalytic work hinges on personal narratives. Stories told need a listener and this chapter is also about listening—even listening to the silence which is always part of the story.

Here is what I think happens: As the journey progresses, the client/patient tells the stories of his life. She tells them in different ways and as she travels she finds old friends and enemies, places and people she had forgotten about, events that stand out, and emotions and fantasies that have been buried or pushed aside. As she gradually puts into words the love and hatred, the envy fueled rage, the fears of separation, the fear of depending, and the pain of unrequited love, laughter, and a new appreciation of life emerge, first in the relationship with one's travel partner and then with others. Scenes shift. New light casts different shadows that reveal and even create new sights. Shame melts with the light. Guilt is diminished. Intimacy becomes possible. Needs change. Talents blossom. Symptoms disappear as strength increases. Along the way the guide or co-traveler is a substitute for past objects but the level playing field helps avoid getting stuck. *"Who me?"* the analyst said when nineteen year old Sam accused him of judging his new girlfriend. *"Could it be that you're mixing me up with your dad."* This sounds corny or less than elegant but we gear our language to the particular patient quite naturally. The idea is to help Sam see and feel the difference. Sometimes we therapists, in our attempts to be neutral forget that being spontaneous and genuine works best.

Terrifying stories come slowly and painfully and usually over a long period of time and when they do, the analyst holds them until the patient becomes strong enough to tolerate expressing them. What helps shift perspective is having the analyst to bounce the stories off. Sometimes she will throw or roll the ball back with a new spin so the story that unfolds gathers new meaning. A new perspective occurs in the safety of the consulting room. Telling a happy story feels dangerous to some patients because they fear that the analyst may think all is well and may end the journey. This is one reason why we are often last to hear about the positive changes in the patient's life.

Stories of child abuse are often acted out and the experienced analyst must listen to her intuition and to other clues that help piece these stories together. The patient who has been continually maltreated often presents as the masochist, reliving the past in hopes of a better outcome. As the therapist listens she enters a new world filled with ideas and emotions. Countertransference (her own transference as I prefer to see it) becomes one important way of knowing her patient. Experiencing fear, sexuality, sadness, despair, elation, in a safe place, the analyst remains present as her partner gains the strength to speak. A co-transference emerges and the dyad learns to step back from time to time in order to understand what goes on. Stories change as they are seen from different perspectives. The therapist may get drawn in too far and enactments occur; but these enactments can be most valuable and can teach both parties when discovered. Listening to and tolerating silence in treatment is also important.

About thirty years ago while teaching a group of clinicians from a free mental health clinic in New Jersey one student presented a case of a young man who never spoke. Because she was in psychoanalytic psychotherapy training she tried her best to draw her young man out but he remained mute. The silence continued week after week for as long as the twelve session class met. The patient came promptly to each session. After several sessions of silence she explained to her patient that this was really hard for her and asked him if he would he mind if she did some paper work. He nodded OK. So she did, looking up occasionally. The class was frustrated by the case and with her. We listened to other cases and each week she would report, "nothing happened." A few months after the course ended she wrote to tell us that Mr. A finally spoke. Seemingly out of the blue he started to talk to her, hesitantly at first, but as she listened to him he began telling her about a trip to the library and eventually about his home life with a disturbed mother and no father. It seems that this man needed time to sit with the therapist and to sense her non-threatening vibe. Although certain situations are not resolvable, just talking to another can be relieving. Without connecting to another, the therapist with the silent man could only imagine what this man's story was but she learned that "not talking" is a message just like anything else. Some would call this resistance but how does that help? Even though psychoanalytic work is called the talking cure, silence has meaning and carries an important message. Sometimes it indicates preverbal trauma, sometimes it alerts the therapist to anxiety, especially if the silence makes her anxious. At times the patient feels pressured. But sometimes silence means relaxation and comfort in a safe place. Tuning in to her own feelings and thoughts can help the therapist get a clue as to what is going on.

The lesson that was reinforced for me and learned by these students is essential in doing psychoanalytic work. We must learn to put our own agendas aside. We have chosen this profession because we want to help people. We all learn different theories and interventions according to the theory we have chosen. But if a patient comes to sessions and for whatever reasons does not speak, the therapist's duty is to wait. This indicates our patience and shows our respect. We cannot impose our needs and wishes on the patient. Other therapists might disagree. After all, it is extremely difficult to sit in silence for weeks. But in this example, the therapist's patience paid off.

Many people believe that psychoanalytic theory is passé. However, in today's world, it is the only treatment that I know of that upholds the patient's right to develop autonomy in a unique and individual way. We are each entitled to have our own values and the psychoanalyst respects this. But there are ways to share our thoughts without imposing them. Aside from the overtly homicidal or suicidal patient the analyst is taught to hold her expectations in abeyance. But common sense, not often mentioned in the psychoanalytic lexicon, is really our most valuable tool. Sometimes common sense tells us to share a story with a particular patient. Such stories emerge spontaneously and often reach the patient more than interpretations do.

Here Ella Sharpe's (1950) words come to mind as they often do so please forgive me for repeating them throughout this book:

> "*The urgency to reform, correct, or make different motivates the task of a reformer or educator, the urgency to cure motivates the physician, but the deep seated interest in people's lives and thoughts must be transformed in the clinician, into an insatiable curiosity, free to range over every field of human experience and activity, free to recognize every unconscious impulse, with only one urgency, namely, a desire to know more, and still more. When we react to something that causes us to think I cannot understand how a person can think or behave like that" curiosity has ceased to be benevolent.*"

The ability to ask "Why" in a genuinely curious manner is what we want to show our patients. I am convinced that in the long run this is the only thing that works. Showing a patient how to be non-judgmentally curious will open up the world for her.

Listening to our patients' stories affords us the opportunity to see and understand how people repeat the influences of the past in the present by living them out. In psychoanalytic work the aim is to talk it out, replacing and/or refining the action. I have said this before but it bears repeating. Any attempt to force the analytic dyad into a shape or to predict an outcome is harmful. Beyond the basic listening and reflective stance of the analyst whose benevolent curiosity guides him, along with the guarantee against boundary crossing, the analyst should not be forced into measuring what transpires. Yes, it is natural to hear things as positive or negative but this must be shared in the dyad. Sometimes we immediately think *uh oh, that was dangerous.* Mary spoke out to her boss in what sounded like a brazen way and later she cringed, worrying that she would be fired. It just so happened that her boss was impressed by her honesty and told her so. So jumping to conclusions must bow to waiting.

Psychoanalytic thinking is not like dentistry or law. It is more like traveling. As one goes along, one begins to understand what happened. Stories are the medium we use to connect.

My first analytic patient, an ex heroin addict, began her story telling me of a wicked witch type mother. As my patient began to see clearly how she tortured her mother—instigating her mother's anger and almost goading her to drink—this mother representation began to change. She began to see her role in that relationship as she repeated it with me. We created our own story that illuminated the original story. But as we went along the lighting shifted. Some aspects got brighter and some receded into the shadows. Good moments appeared in the treatment and also in memories of the mother. Bad moments lost their place in the spotlight. We learned how and why the early story was written in her mind and in a way, it was edited and embellished during our work together. By seeing her mother as wicked, C. felt entitled to behave seductively with her father by making him an ally. She could ignore her competitive feelings with mother by denigrating her. Her wish for father's attention seemed justified thereby avoiding the recognition of her own guilt. But she expressed that guilt by injuring herself. In analysis she began to understand why she was accident prone.

Time after time, from the clinic to private practice and equally when when supervising, I have witnessed people translate the action into words. The articulation of trauma, fantasy, rage, and love are change agents.

One major problem for the psychoanalyst is connecting, not only with the patient but to the public. Most people think psychoanalysis is passé and are surprised to know that couches are still around, available, and sometimes useful. The books I have mentioned and will now discuss have captured my interest over the years—books that could enlighten the public. They are about everyday people written in accessible, jargon free prose—books that could help people understand what psychoanalysis is for and about and even how it looks. In my mind, the public has held an unfortunate picture of this work and it is the analyst's responsibility to make the work understood. What better way than by writing. Explaining how we work by using the story telling aspect of psychoanalysis is crucial to the growth of our profession. Other forms of treatment focus on specific problems and although this can be helpful, with long standing issues that involve intimacy, loneliness, and inhibition, a non-judgmental, long term approach is necessary.

The manner in which stories are told varies but the basic stance of the analyst is benevolent curiosity. It is this kind of curiosity that can open doors to a freer life, a life with new choices. Loewald

(1960) legitimized the concept of the analyst as new object whose ability to listen is often a new experience in a patient's life. Being listened to means being paid attention. If you think about it, how often have you been really listened to for any length of time? A psychoanalyst can have all sorts of knowledge and experience but each patient has a unique story that will aid them in their pursuit to find out what lies beneath their problems.

What are the *real true* stories? There aren't any. All stories are based on individual perception over time. There is no such thing as real when it comes to memory. As perception changes from second to second and minute to minute and year to year our views change. We look at a painting from one angle and when we move it looks different. We listen to music while in one mood and hear it differently in a different mood. We tell a story one day and the next day we tell it differently. So the analyst must be flexible enough to go with the changes. The very process of expressing memories changes them. The past is revised and the brain changes. The result can be enormous, even mind-boggling but it happens so slowly that we may not even notice it. It's something like growing taller. We just don't notice as it's happening.

Newell Fischer (2019), in *Nine Lives* (which I often call Nine Loves) tells us about nine very different people, men and women and a teen-age boy and how they presented him with difficult problems. Each chapter tells a story that is followed by the author's comments.

"Henry felt as if he were "sleepwalking" through life." "Something is wrong with me..I'm missing life...I feel like I'm half dead." The story unfolds and we learn that Henry, at age 8, had repressed or split off

the witnessing of his father's massive heart attack while sleeping next to him on the eve of a fishing trip. All Henry remembered was being disappointed about the cancellation of the trip (memory can be used to screen other memories). From that time on Henry lived a "muted" and lonely life. During his analysis, Henry repeated the trauma of his father's death by sleeping through many of his sessions. *"Day after day he "died" on my couch and I had to revive him."* says Fischer. In the comments after the story Fischer tells the reader how even before the trauma Henry had developed a kind of defensive withdrawal. Enacting it in analysis was the beginning of change. We learn that before the trauma Henry had developed a 'half-asleep' approach to life due to his mother's unpredictable outbursts during which his father remained aloof and unavailable. I suspect that one aspect of Henry's sleepwalking through life, not mentioned by Fischer, had to do with his rage at Father who did not protect him. Rather than face the possibility that he wished his father dead, he lived a life in the shadows and when he did emerge, after years of analysis, he volunteered as an EMT worker.

"Like a sandstorm, Mary blew into my psychotherapeutic practice, blinded me, caused disruption, and disappeared" begins the story of a delusional woman who intruded on Fischer's life in a drastically dramatic way. But with all the trouble she caused, Fischer manages to explain his understanding of Mary's delusional world with empathy, explaining the causes and even the adaptive aspect of her solution.

"My treatment of Diana was a failure ..." is the beginning of Chapter Seven and we learn how a patient's suicide after several years of analysis is explained and experienced by the analyst. I tended to

second guess this treatment which I see as my own reaction to the suicide. Diana had drained several previous therapists when Newell agreed to see her six times a week for over four years, with intermittent hospitalizations due to suicidal threats. It was an act of heroism in my opinion. Diana's story was a tragic one of abandonment and neglect that explained her rage and despair and one must consider if holding out hope with analysis is not another opportunity for the experience of failure on both sides. But Newell's treatment of Diana speaks to his character. Marilyn Monroe was such a case and her analyst, Ralph Greenson, was blamed by some for her suicide (if it was a suicide). Greenson crossed boundaries, and Fischer did not. Fischer mentions Diana's disease as evolving from a deficiency problem to a malabsorbtion disease. But Diana's suicide note ending with *"please don't be angry with me"* tells us more accurately what she felt while breaking our hearts at the same time. In essence, Diana was expressing her murderous rage and Fischer was one of the casualties. The analyst's rescue wishes blend with the responsibility he feels. At such times failure is not unusual. There seemed to be no choices for Diana or Fisher. We are offered a glimpse of the work where he describes how in the third year Diana refused to speak for three months. *"Sometimes ...I tried to put into words what I thought was going on in her mind—her anger at me, her attempt to isolate herself and protect herself from her thoughts, and her efforts to drive me away. At other times we sat in silence."* says Newell. We are told that after sessions Diana wrote to Dr. Fischer (one hundred letters during the three month period) describing in exquisite detail her inner thoughts and feelings. I was deeply moved by this chapter and by Fischer's ability to stay with it. Someone was there for Diana and that fact makes the work truly heroic. Diana's tragedy had begun in utero, continued throughout life, and ended in suicide but the several years in treatment must have shown her that someone cared. Unfortunately it was not enough.

Each chapter in *Nine Lives* illustrates the tragedies of life and how they do or do not respond to a connection with this analyst. No reader will be left without questions—and all readers will learn just how this analyst works: with knowledge, patience, and deep compassion.

Stephan Grosz's book *The Examined Life: How We Lose and Find Ourselves* is quite another experience yet fascinating in its own way. Grosz writes like a good short story/mystery author. Nice descriptions, a fast pace, to the point, and concise. As an analyst I found his descriptions a bit slick at times but entertaining and very useful. Grosz's premise is that if one cannot tell his story, his story will tell him. This makes real sense and the psychoanalyst is the person who will try her hardest to welcome that story. In one chapter Peter shocks those around him. Pretending suicide a few times, Peter finds his way to Mr. Grosz who takes him into analysis. Known for leaving people and jobs abruptly, Peter repeats this habit in order to shock his analyst who receives a letter from Peter's fiancee announcing his death by suicide. Mr Grosz sends a condolence note and receives a thank you note. End of story? No. Six months later Mr. Grosz receives a message from Peter. Stunned, shocked, confused, he and Peter resume analysis. The dyad learns that in his first two years Peter had been severely abused by his parents and learned to avoid dependency at all costs and that his habit of abruptly leaving others was his way of letting them feel for him by experiencing the way he felt. This story ends well enough and is an illustration of how Peter coped. The lay public might well learn that life can be complicated and mysterious and even solvable. Grosz shows us that anything can happen in this work.

Chapters are divided into five sections: Beginnings, Telling Lies, Loving, Changing, and Leaving. In the Changing section we see more of how analysis works. Grosz has a unique way of describing what goes on by using others' as well as his own techniques. But more illuminating is his description of what one analysand went through. On Being a Patient we meet Tom, an old friend of Grosz's. Over lunch Tom talks about what he has experienced in his treatment. We hear about his compulsions and his difficulty in sharing them with his analyst. Grosz, by letting his friend recap his analysis, tells us more about the actual process of analysis than he does in the rest of his book.

Susie Orbach's (1999) book *The Impossibility of Sex* is refreshing. Upfront she tells us that her cases are fictional. Many case histories in our literature are indeed fictionalized—and certainly do not provide scientific evidence but they can still teach us. This book is beautifully written and takes the reader inside the analyst's head. It also presents the theories she calls on to substantiate her work. In her chapter about the erotic transference for instance, she takes the reader along, step by step, as she analyzes a man who comes close to seducing her. She shares her countertransference and her real attractions to this patient and tells exactly how she maintained her analytic stance. *"Adam was a fornicator, a lover, a stud: a man whose daily life was shaped by sexual desire and sexual conquest..."* who sought therapy when he *"had to ejaculate too soon." "Too soon for whom"* asks Orbach and Adam's story unfolds.

In a chapter called Footsteps in the Dark about an abused patient who in mid-treatment brought a knife to the office, Orbach says: *"There are moments in almost every therapy when the known suddenly evaporates ..."*

This book is useful for the analyst as Orbach imagines her countertransference in what seem like unusual situations but entirely plausible at the same time. Her writing is clear, jargon free and instructive. Her imaginary treatments go into far greater depth unlike the Fischer and Grosz books. Orbach's book tells a patient's story and a therapist's inner reactions and how they are used in service of the treatment. And there's more. She inserts in italics how she makes use of theory. I found her use of people like Winnecott, Sandler, Lacan, Person, Mahler, Bollas, and Freud to shore up her thinking, educative and sensible and always readable. I would add this book to all psychoanalytically based curricula as it a great teaching tool on countertransference and the therapist's use of herself to understand what can happen in treatment.

In sum, I highly recommend that analytic education include Grosz, Fischer, and Orbach in their curricula.

I once assigned Toni Morison's (1987) *Beloved* in a class on unconscious fantasy. This haunting novel describes loss and mourning in exquisite detail—more than any book or article I have seen. Reading these books allows us to remember that people are unique and cannot be pigeonholed into diagnostic categories where they stop breathing.

Novels and memoirs can be read with a psychoanalytic eye just as music can be listened to with a psychoanalytic ear.

Enjoy!

CHAPTER 12

MARTIN BERGMANN INTERVIEW

"What the teacher is, is more important than what he teaches."
— Karl A. Menninger

My decision to share the following interview with Martin Bergmann as the last chapter of this collection is meant as a tribute to him. And, like the first chapter, it is about love. In my opinion, no one exuded the love of life and work as Martin did, and I shall always remember him for that rare quality.

Prelude

Martin Bergmann definitely had charisma. A tall, fit man with a good sense of humor, a twinkle in his eye, a European accent, a gift for extemporaneous speaking, and a fount of knowledge, combined with genuine enthusiasm made him a favorite teacher of hundreds of students, including myself. He conducted daily seminars for psychoanalytic clinicians and thinkers and these groups lasted for many years with only occasional new members when someone left making space available. The classes varied in size and were organized and run by students. One had to be invited by a member of a particular group and then voted on. I shall always be grateful to my friend and colleague Ed Fancher for my invitation. I was very lucky. The Friday group I joined had been meeting for many years and was considered to be his advanced seminar. I remember many intellectually stimulating discussions, both theoretical and clinical. I was somewhat intimidated at first but the group was not a competitive one, as many are, and I attributed this to the tone Martin set. He never presented himself as all-knowing despite his vast knowledge and the fact that he had the whole history of psychoanalysis in his head. With all of his knowledge I experienced him as genuinely open-minded. He was never critical and if someone was out of the ball park he found ways to respond that were not hurtful. Rather than frantically raising our hands when wanting to contribute, Martin would go around the room, giving everyone a chance to speak. Over the years the students, many of whom were teachers themselves, decided on various topics of study such as narcissism, sadomasochism, depression, using the relevant literature. Fifteen or twenty of us met every Friday from noon to two in the living room of Martin and Maria's beautiful Fifth Avenue apartment, sitting on couches and comfortable chairs. Years later I attended a smaller seminar that met in the dining room. What I learned from Martin has deeply affected my own style of thinking and teaching. His references to the uniqueness of patient and analyst made complete sense to me and profoundly affected my development as an analyst. Martin always said that every book or article has something useful, even if you disagree with the basic premise. Most meaningful to me was his enthusiasm. He has inspired so many in the field and it is a real pleasure to present an interview that I recorded on February 10, 2008 in his beautiful office with its view of Central Park and the Hudson River. But first I will share parts of an earlier interview from twenty years earlier, in 1988.

JH: We have covered some of the past and the present. Here are a few short one-liners to do with the future. If I had the time tomorrow I would...

MB: I will answer you paradoxically. I think as one gets older death becomes one last Oedipal rival. One knows he will defeat you eventually, but one tries to fight him off as long as possible. There is a Jewish legend that always meant a lot to me: The angel of death came to take Moses but Moses said to him "You've got to wait until I have finished my five books" and the angel of death sat outside the tent waiting for him to finish. Is that an answer to your question?

JH: That's lovely—I like that. A book that I plan to re-read...

MB: There are many, many, many such books. I would say that if I had the time I would re-read all the books that I read during my adolescence, that I haven't read for many years, and try to see what's in them for me now. I remember when I was eighteen I wrote in my diary that there is nothing left to write about because Dostoevsky and Kafka have said it all. I would like to re-read them and see.

JH: A subject that has always interested me and that I have not explored has to do with....

MB: Oh yes, there are many, again there are many, many. In a way I think that a seminar I teach is really only good for me if I uncover during the seminar that I have to write the next paper. I feel that I ought to write a paper on reconstruction, because I have a very different idea than the seminar that I attended. The course I give now is one on fantasy and I have realized that Freud was unambivalent about dreams but very ambivalent about fantasy. As a result, the fantasy never received the status in psychoanalysis that it should have and although Arlow did a great deal on that subject, I have a different take on it. So that would be another subject I would like to write about. I would also like to write about psychoanalysis and social reality because I have a feeling (that also grew out of my holocaust book and my my work with anti-semitism) that we don't do justice to the social reality of psychoanalysis itself within institutions and the way such social reality affects our work. That interests me. There are many more subjects. One of my ambitions is to write a second edition to my love book because I feel I understand much more than when I wrote it. That happens each time when you finish a book; you want another one. Right now the book is going to appear in a paper back edition. I owe to a large extent the popularity of this rather difficult book to the laudatory review by Donald Kaplan.

JH: Do you have some advice for the beginning psychoanalyst?

MB: Yes I do. You see in my day what was relatively easy was that there was no conflict about the model. There were actually two models. The model of Freud and the model of Hartmann. But we were not bright enough to know that Hartmann fundamentally changed the model. That occurred to me only much later. There was a Melanie Klein who was in S.A and England that we did not have to worry about. So basically we were confronted only with one model. I think the young analyst of today, whether they like it or not, is confronted with a multiplicity of models. If he decided to join a particular organization, he can be sure that he will be subjected, perhaps mercilessly, to the the one model and would be discouraged from interest in the other models. I would urge the opposite. I would urge that you learn very much about your own model but afterwards explore the other models available because you always learn something from them. That is I don't regard any deviate school as having nothing to contribute.

JH: That is what is so rare about your teaching.

MB: That is probably what is characteristic of my teaching. In other words, I think there is something to be learned, only we have to understand the historical conditions that give rise to a model and forgive the extremes to which it went.

JH: I'm so glad you ended with this because it is the way that we began and what's so wonderful about studying with you that you always find something of value. Thank you, Martin.

Interview of Martin Bergmann by Jane Hall February 10, 2008

Hall: It has been frequently said that the analysis and the supervision are far more important in education than the classes. In my mind teaching is an art, and can be inspiring in a way that supervision and analysis cannot. Martin, I would like this interview to focus on your teaching experience over the years, the fact that you have had full seminars, every week day, for over how many years?

Bergmann: I started teaching in 1953. It is over fifty years. Not quite sixty years.

Hall: A long time! You have taught more people in the field of psychoanalysis than any single teacher in any institute. Will you tell me how this came about, and what your inspirations have been and are today?

Bergmann: Maybe the many questions that you are asking me I will try to free associate to them. First of all, I think that the teaching of psychoanalysis basically consists of two types of teaching. The first one I would compare to cutting the stones for a mason to build a house. The second one is more architectural, similar to building the house out of the raw materials that have been assembled. Now, the raw materials consist of knowing such things as psychosexual phases, the transformation of the various psychosexual phases into character traits, the variations on the Oedipus complex, the positive oedipus, the negative oedipus, and the combining of the two into the total Oedipus complex, those are the basic stones that every student has to know about. Those are on the whole, though they evoke some resistances, are teachable. What is less easy to teach is the art of interpretation. Or as Freud preferred to call it sometimes, reconstruction. Because even if you know all the basic ingredients of psychoanalysis, how to make the interpretation, particularly a creative interpretation and not just a translation of what you learn in school, is very difficult. The tripartite division… I assume that the most likely place to learn how to interpret other people is in your own analysis. In your analysis you can learn to interpret someone who happens to be similar to you. But what if you encounter somebody built fundamentally different? Then how to reconstruct is an art, which is essentially transmitted by the supervising therapists, however, no guidelines to these supervisors has ever been given in a meaningful sense. In other words, we don't really know how to help somebody to make a coherent interpretation which is based on the uniqueness of the patient.

This brings up another point that I would like to emphasize. Freud was interested in creating a science. A science is based on repetitive phenomena. Science does not prepare us for the unique and special, at least not in an obvious way. So that, to some extent, Freud's eagerness to have psychoanalysis recognized as a science tended to work against the recognition of the uniqueness of the analyst and the uniqueness of the patient. For example, when we say this person has been analyzed well, how much does it tell us? This depends on him and her as a patient and on the analyst. One analysis is not basically similar to the next. So that this is why on the whole how to teach the art of interpretation has become difficult.

Hall: Do you feel though, that the classes that you teach are of equal value to supervision, in a different way, and how? Because I have studied with you, as have many others, and we keep coming back. Something happens in your classes that is different from working with a supervisor, and certainly different from analysis. It is exciting and stimulating and I wondered what is your thought on how exciting class work can be?

Bergmann: Well you know when I first started in 1953, my aim was really to replicate the work of the institute that excluded non-medical analysts. That was the aim and that kept me for quite a time. But after the changes, and institutes were willing to accept non-medical members and also some medical members that were not accepted, the whole tenor of my teaching substantially changed. It used to be modeled after the institute, but once the institutes were created they took on a different character depending on the people who are there. I, usually at the end of each semester, ask each group what they would like to do. And then if I am not ready to teach what they ask me to teach, I read during the summer and prepare for it. But I usually try to follow what the classes have suggested. As a result of that, particularly if the group develops a social cohesion, the classes just go on and I continue to learn.

Hall: Yes, I was in a seminar with you for about 5 years. It was a large group and I learned so much. You always told us to get something positive from an article even if we did not like it. There was some turn over in members but not much.

Bergmann: Individual members leave and others come, but the classes go on, sometimes as long as twenty years.

Hall: That is really impressive.

Bergmann: As the classes continue they become more exploration. My advanced classes are much more exploratory than teaching what institutes usually give and many of my students are teachers themselves, so that gives it a whole different connotation.

Hall: Has there been a shift in the interest of the seminars, are students more eclectic today since the advent of self psychology and relational theory, or did some of the groups chose just one theory of mind and keep reading about that?

Bergmann: Now you are asking a very important question. I will take some time to answer it. In the past, people would agree or disagree with Freud. What is happening today is that as we move further and further away from Freud, there is neither agreement or disagreement. The students today, or many students today, no longer understand Freud. So that I have to reiterate it in a language which is a little closer to them. This is particularly true with certain difficult books like *The Ego and the Id.* One has to read it almost line by line because the book is no longer accessible. So the teacher has a fundamentally different task, and that is to act as a bridge between the students and what Freud said.

Then the teacher has another task. In my opinion Freud did not understand himself very well. Or at least, didn't understand himself in the way in which I understand him. And I now have to convey to the students my understanding. So what is an example? It seems to me that it is important to convey this to the students from the very beginning. Freud was a man who changed his mind twice. And twice in his life he built up a completely, or at least reasonably, different theory. Now most models don't do that. Most models are satisfied with one theory that meets their needs. The first transformation took place between 1895 and 1900 from the cathartic model to the topographic model. Because we have the Fliess letters available, this transformation can be taught and is documented. But to my great surprise, when you give the Fliess letters to a student today, they shock the student. The students do not know how to deal with them. There Freud explains to Fliess, who is like a reluctant follower, what psychoanalysis is all about and he tries to convince Fliess. But the student who is reading it without guidance fails to understand the atmosphere and the whole connection. We have to explain to our students the difference between the cathartic model and the topographic model. Then after twenty years, the same thing happens all over again and Freud makes a major transition from the topographic to the structural. Here we are less well informed as to why Freud did this. And the transition is much more difficult so that you have to explain to the student the difference between topographic and the structural. Those are general introductory notes or understanding that a student must get in terms of an overall picture before one gets into the details and the nitty-gritty of psychoanalysis. Then to teach the art of interpretation, such as Freud suggested in the 1937 paper *On Construction* that is again a different endeavor and requires a completely different approach.

Hall: What do you say though that some of us, anyway, still are using the topographical model? We talk about the unconscious more than we talk about the superego sometimes.

Bergmann: Well you see, that is an important point to know. Freud never thought in *The Ego and Id*, or in any other place, that the structural should replace the topographic. He always saw the structural as adding complexity to the topographic, but he didn't see this as two distinct methods. Arlow's and Brenner's success was to demonstrate how different they are and why in their view the structural is superior to the topographic. This influenced American psychoanalysis in a certain way. I think that this is diminishing somewhat now, but it has given a cast to American psychoanalysis for a whole generation.

Hall: What do you prefer to teach? Do you like to teach the theory that we have just been talking about or do you like to teach clinical material?

Bergmann: I think if I have any preference it is to teach the combination of the two, because that is what makes psychoanalysis. Excessive theorizing is kind of Talmudic.

Hall: If you were a student today, just starting out, where would you find the best education in psychoanalysis? Would you find it in the institute or would you find it in private seminars where the students could select different teachers for long periods of time?

Bergmann: I would hate to answer that question.

Hall: (laugh)

Bergmann: It seems the institutes are necessary for teaching all of the fundamentals. The other part can be done with a teacher or even in peer groups. Those are different tasks. One task is to train a student to become a therapist, the other task helps him to continue to grow and be productive.

Hall: Do you think that Arlow was right when he once said that Freud's cases should not be taught, in the beginning anyway, because they would confuse the students?

Bergmann: That is a problem. Because the cases used to be taught as examples of what one should do. The teacher can show how brilliant Freud was in many ways, but also how mistaken he was. If he teaches the case, not as something to follow, but as something to understand how psychoanalysis developed, it can lead to a very good historical understanding.

Hall: Which of Freud's papers do you think a student, a beginning student, should read first?

Bergmann: Now that is a very interesting question, and I would say as we are getting further and further from Freud that the International actually ought to appoint a committee that will do just what you are asking me to do. That must be a collective decision based on more collective wisdom.

If I were asked, I probably would begin with the 1909 Freud's *Clark Lectures*. And then I would go to the *Introductory Lectures*, again covering the same material in a kind of concise way. I would see then how my class is doing, and from there one would have to branch out to whatever the class is weakest at.

Hall: Okay, this brings me to the classes. When you teach, which is almost all the time, how do you manage to connect so powerfully with the students? Is it your love of teaching, love of psychoanalysis, your love for those who wish to learn?

Bergmann: All the three together.

Hall: Because you do have that gift that many people don't have.

Bergmann: Well you see, I have a certain advantage. My father was a professor of a university and when I was an adolescent in Jerusalem he took me every week to a workers' seminar where he taught philosophy and I saw him teach. And then when he left, some students would follow him and ask questions and I would listen. At some point my Father would say to his students: "From now on I want to talk to my son." The students would be sent away and my father would ask me what I thought. So that was a kind of precious preparation that not everybody has.

Hall: Absolutely. That's where the love comes from.

Bergmann: Maybe.

Hall: I think so. That's really exciting. Martin, do you often hear people say, "That's an interesting idea, let me think about it." Or "Maybe you have a point, I think perhaps I have overlooked that." I am particularly interested if people can change their minds.

Bergmann: Andre Green once said that he never heard an analyst change his or her mind.

Hall: So, do you believe that analysts are flexible, and since we are talking about you, are you flexible and open to different ways of listening to patients and students? In other words, do you have an open mind or are you pretty definite?

Bergmann: I don't think an analyst exists that considers his mind closed. His mind may be closed but he thinks he is open. But let me try to answer it in a somewhat different way.

Hall: Okay.

Bergmann: It is really amazing that now I will be 95 in a week, so the fact is that even now I encounter patients such as I have never seen. So that I always learn something new. And so, that for me, to repeat what I know, and I may like to repeat it once or twice, the third time it is kind of boring. What is really interesting is that my students teach me something new or teach me to explain the old in a different way so that ours is really an ever interesting, growing profession. And that's why I thank my audiences for having saved me from the swimming pools of Florida.

Hall: (laughs) But there is a school now that calls themselves the relational school, and there is another school of self psychology. And if you get a more Freudian group, or a more classical or whatever you want to call it, Bionian, do you see those people clinging to their theories? Those are the people I wonder about closed mindedness. They hear a different theory and they refuse to say, "Well, maybe this is a different way of looking at it."

Bergmann: Well, very often the work of analysis itself becomes a kind of quasi-religion. You can be orthodox, then you are like your analyst, or you can be mad at your analyst and then you become a protestant and you acquire a different attitude. But in either way you are as dogmatic as you could be.

Hall: But don't you think there is something in between? In other words, shouldn't an analyst find his or her own voice, not his or her analysts's voice, not the supervisor's voice, but a combination of those voices and other voices and their own voice, how they metabolize what they have heard?

Bergmann: There is absolutely no doubt that any creative analyst must do that. But I think that history can be helpful here. You ought to know the stages that Freud himself went through and then you ought to know this is a matter of disagreement, but in my opinion one is a better analyst if one also knows a little bit what Kleinians do or what Kohutians do not necessarily to be a Kleinian but to say to yourself "Oh, this patient would have been ideal for Melanie Klein and that patient would have done very well with Kohut." And then you can try to see what you can borrow from those others that is useful. Because in a way, every dissenter to some extent had grounds for dissent. And here, if you will allow me, I am going to tell you another favorite idea of mine. And this is: under the topographic model, where what is repressed was relatively small and the repression could be undone in a couple of months, analyses ended and it was a pleasure to be an analyst. Under the structural model it is a much more complicated issue, victory is much less certain, and the whole thing is a much more difficult endeavor. So that in a way, today, we don't think that anybody has been completely analyzed. We only say that the analysis, if it was successful, prepared the road for self-analysis. So that analysis does not end, it is converted into self-analysis at a certain point. But if you watch self-analysis, you see two types. Sometimes the former analysand remains grateful to his analyst. But if the self-analysis goes far, or goes significantly beyond the analysis, what I call by the Greek word hubris, pride, sets in.

Hall: (Sighs)

Bergmann: And at that point the temptation to start a new school gets overwhelming. So, either you discovered something beyond your analysis that in your opinion nobody has ever discovered, what is to prevent you from becoming like Freud, heading a new movement? The identification with Freud leads to imitation. Then you start a new school. So there is something inherent in the analytic process itself which in my opinion is conducive to different schools and will be conducive to it in the future.

Hall: So, why do you think that the schools can't somehow integrate more, instead of being so split off, with so called different schools. Why can't eventually we embrace different ways of thinking and experiencing without splitting into different schools? Why can't the past be used in conjunction with the here and now, for instance?

Bergmann: Because of the aggressive drive.

Hall: Really. Can you tell me about that?

Bergmann: This is a lovely picture that you portrayed. But no board of any analytic school will be willing to stop teaching their way and be willing to send their best students to a general psychoanalytic school. That is asking for more than ordinary human beings are capable of sacrificing.

Hall: Okay, but that is my interest. Why have we become so comfortable with the aggressiveness that we all have, even when you talk politics or anything else, why do we not let more libido out? Why can we not respect each other and hear each other out? Like today there are debates on the presidency where they speak against each other instead of speaking for their own ideas. Why can't people be more respectful? Why do they have to do things like tear each other down instead of coming up with ideas, and incorporate somebody's idea and see if that could work? Why is the aggression so easy? And the libido so difficult to express?

Bergmann: What you are saying makes you a lovely woman. You would like libido to rule the world.

Hall: But do you think that is naive?

Bergmann: In Freud's dual instinct theory, yes. Aggression is here, the question is what we do with it. And maybe to transform it into schools that fight each other is better than throwing stones at each other.

Hall: Well, I am still confused about that.

Bergmann: No, you are not confused, you are utopian.

Hall: Well, or maybe it is a reaction formation, I don't know.

Bergmann: No, a reaction formation sounds different.

Hall: Okay .

Bergmann: No, this is, I think, lovely only it is unrealizable. From where would you get the energy to spend so much time in committee meetings if it were not also satisfaction of some derivatives of the aggressive drive.

Hall: Well, there are always derivatives of the aggressive drive, but I don't see as many libidinal derivatives in discussions.

Bergmann: That's what Freud was afraid of in *The Ego and the Id*, that is why he wrote *Civilization and its Discontents*, and that's why he worried, and rightly so, about the future of mankind. The aggressive drive is a serious obstacle, and once the aggressive in the structural phase when the role of the death instinct and aggression was recognized psychoanalysis was no longer allied with the progressive, messianic groups of the twentieth century, of which I hear you would like to be a member.

Hall: (Laughs) Well, I'm not sure. For instance, Trudy Blank used to say when we would talk about aggression and libido, "the aggressive drive helps you walk out the door" or helps you move. But why isn't it the libidinal drive? You know, you want to go greet somebody, that's libido, that's not aggression.

Bergmann: No, but libido aims at union, not separation.

Hall: Yes?

Bergmann: She was right. The aggressive drive separates us. The libido drive makes us embrace each other.

Hall: Well, I would like to see a little more of that. (Laughs)

Bergmann: You would like to see that... Okay.

Hall: I guess it starts, though, in the cradle. Or do you think it is genetic?

Bergmann: We know that the cradle has a lot to do with how strongly libido will be vis-a-vis aggression. But no cradle is loving enough to raise a child without aggression.

Hall: I understand that aggression is necessary.

Bergmann: Well, but we have a little bit more than absolutely necessary. We could do with a great deal less and the world still would go wrong.

Hall: (Laughs) Okay, one question I didn't write down. What do you think that people like about Bion, and I can't think of anybody else right now but Bion seems to be so popular these days.

There are study groups that are going on, Bionian, which I don't understand, but I feel I probably should know more about this.

Bergmann: Why should you?

Hall: Well, because, you know, if it helps understand people. Is it just a different language?

Bergmann: Well, this is another issue. You see, sometimes the same terms are given another name. Therefore, what Freud held against Adler was that Adler took Freud's concepts and gave them different names. That is a part of the aggressive drive, now allied with narcissism. If I give something known a different name, I get famous.

Hall: Right.

Bergmann: So from that point of view, it is worth it, but then you have to sell it.

Hall: Yes.

Bergmann: And sometimes you are successful and sometimes you are not. Now for example you are saying you should know Bion. But you are not saying why you should. What is it that you don't understand about your patients that you think Bion could help you with?

Hall: Truthfully, I think I am understanding my patients through my own ears and my own experience. But, if my experience included something about Bion, I don't know, would I hear them better?
Bergmann: Well, give Bion a chance, read a couple of pages. And see if he is worth it.

Hall: (laughs) We had a meeting last year called The Future of Psychoanalytic Education. Arnie Richards and I were the co-chairs.

Bergmann: Okay.

Hall: We invited people from every institute, every umbrella group, from the Jungians to Spotnitzians±you name it, everybody, and we had mixed panels. We invited Jurgen Reeder to give the keynote. He wrote the book *Hate and Love in Analytic Institutes*. It was the first time that I know of that we had this kind of ecumenical meeting, where everybody participated... and what we did was encourage people from the audience to speak. We limited the papers to ten minutes and the audience was really the focus. And the feeling was so wonderful. People felt so good being included. Included by whom, I don't know, because we were all people from different institutes and places. Even this group called NAAP, which is upsetting everybody because of the new licensing law, participated. So to me that is sort of fighting the aggressive stance.

Bergmann: I suspect that if you had lasted a little longer you would have seen these groups argue more. Of course the joy to be included is overwhelming. We all love to be loved. After a while you would have heard from the other component.

Hall: Yes, okay. So then we come to the politics of exclusion which are so rampant. It started when psychoanalysis came to this country, and the medical people claimed it as their own, and then other people excluded others, and the other people carried on the tradition of exclusion. There is always excluding.

Bergmann: But when I wish to be included and I am included there is no guarantee that I won't say, "Well, now that am I included, it is time to exclude." Because there is the wish to belong, but the wish also not to let anybody in.

Hall: So does that happen in a classroom? I have never known you to exclude an interested student if they want to learn, unless you have no room in you seminars. I want to get back to the teaching and exclusion within the class. Sometimes students get annoyed at one student.

Bergmann: That happens many times. The class combines against a particular member of the class and wants the teacher to do something about it.

Hall: So what happens then?

Bergmann: You explain to the class that this is the phenomenon of aggression and if you exclude this culprit another culprit will appear.

Hall: (laughs)

Bergmann: So we might as well deal with this culprit.

Hall: There is always a culprit.

Bergmann: I remember that I realized this in the army. Every company had to have a scapegoat. But who was chosen as the scapegoat was determined by certain psychological conditions.

Hall: Masochism?

Bergmann: Masochism, intelligence, not fighting back. There are certain things.

Hall: Some classes want the teacher to intervene when someone takes too much time. And in my experience, some students appreciate an all knowing teacher and others seem ready to think on their own.

Bergmann: I suppose when you are anxious you want somebody authoritarian. So when you are not anxious, you prefer somebody who is less dogmatic, it depends on the state of anxiety.

Hall: How do you see the future of psychoanalytic education? Do you think that, for instance, this new TV program *In Treatment* will interest more people? Have you seen it?

Bergmann: I heard about it.

Hall: I wonder if that is going to interest people to liven up the field, or if you have any thoughts about that? Can we predict that analysis will flourish again?

Bergmann: The reason why I know that you can't predict is that because at no stage in analysis could one predict its future. If I would know how to predict I would write a text. But, it is impossible to know when a Melanie Klein will show up, or when the situation in the world will change as it did after World War II, so analysis usually cannot be predicted without an understanding of the future of civilization. How interested will we be in introspection? Let's assume that the medical industry will be successful in creating a pill against every conceivable mental illness. What will happen then? Will everybody choose pills, or will there be somebody who will say, "I want to understand myself rather than to just suppress all this inconvenience."

It is very hard to predict because we don't know the future analysts and we don't know the next stage in the development of culture.

Hall: What do you think about the word charisma? How can you explain why one person has charisma and another person doesn't?

Bergmann: We do know something about charisma. A charismatic person has a certain inner certainty about himself, who he is, and where he stands. He has himself gone through an experience where he gained a new kind of certainty. So a charismatic person has gone through some development that makes him feel that he has something to offer and when he believes in that he sometimes finds followers. It doesn't mean that he is great, because charisma seems to obscure the fact that there is a difference between a Hitler and a Gandhi.

Hall: Yes.

Bergmann: They both have charisma but it is a charisma of a different kind.

Hall: What do you think Gandhi was about? I mean, there was man who was not aggressive. He was passive.

Bergmann: Well, that's not quite true. In certain ways he was very aggressive. He was a complex person. What he advocated was something which the British Empire could not withstand. A Gandhi versus a Hitler would never have amounted to much. So it is always a reciprocal relationship between the person and the culture.

Hall: Okay, another question. You are a wonderful extemporaneous speaker, I never saw you read a paper. Do you write that way, when you write a book or an article?

Bergmann: When I write a book?

Hall: Do you write, or do you speak into a tape recorder?

Bergmann: I never speak in that I always write it.

Hall: How do you explain that? Because you speak so beautifully on the spot. Is it a different part of your brain that you use?

Bergmann: Yes. For example, what you asked me today were not questions that I had fundamentally to think about. Here and there was a little surprise. But if I want to write something, I want to say something new and I want to make sure that I understood what already has been said about the subject.

Hall: Who would you say has been your greatest inspiration, aside from Freud?

Bergmann: Aside from Freud?

Hall: Right.

Bergman: In my life or in my analysis?

Hall: Who comes to mind first?

Bergmann: First comes Freud, then comes nothing.

Hall: Wow. (laughs) Well, your father.

Bergmann: My father, that is in a different sphere.

Hall: Because I think he inspired your teaching.

Bergmann: Well, you brought that out of me today but I didn't think about it before.

Hall: Oh?

Bergmann: Who do I value highly? I would say certainly Andre Green, certain aspects of Kris, certain aspects of Kernberg. You know it all depends. I don't worship anybody, including Freud. I have learned this or that from various authors, but I wouldn't ask myself who is more influential.

Hall: And what are you reading now, for your own pleasure or your own interest, aside from what you do for your classes?

Bergmann: My wife and I are trying to write a book about the opera and that occupies me. Not so long ago I wrote, with my son, a book about Shakespeare's sonnets, so that occupied me for a while.

Hall: I'd like to go back to being authoritarian and how some institutes impose their way of thinking on the students. Does this affect the candidates approach to the patient? For instance, if we are learning about the transference neurosis or penis envy or whatever, is the student then going to impose that and affect the patient?

Bergmann: That is the trouble I saw that Freud got us into. You see, he thought that the era of discovery was already behind him. He and Abraham and Ferenzci made the great discoveries, and thought that now you could just teach analysts by letting them know what you have acquired. That was a very serious mistake.

Hall: Yes.

Bergmann: So to some extent Freud sanctioned the idea that you just tell the patient what you have learned in your school. But there is this very interesting story of Greenson's patient who dreamt that the analyst took a suit from the rack and he wanted the analyst to create an original suit for him. Our patients know very well whether we are understanding them or if we are delivering to them what we have learned. That is very important, to teach our future analysts not to always use standard interpretations.

Hall: Absolutely. I had a patient recently who has a very precocious, bright three-year-old little girl. Both parents adore this little girl and the mother was talking about the toilet training and how all the child's friends are toilet trained. And she says, "I don't push her, I just let her do whatever . . whatever happens, she knows where the potty is and so on. Now, I know this patient very well, and I know about her childhood, and so I wondered with her whether she had some thoughts about this, and whether because she is rather independent and rebellious, if any of her thoughts have been picked up by her daughter. "Absolutely not, absolutely not. That is so from the book!" she said. Now, you could say I took that from what I have learned, but her dismissal of it was so vehement.

Bergmann: That is a reaction formation. What you said before was not.

Hall: Yes, exactly. Okay.

Bergmann: "Absolutely not" is a reaction formation.

Hall: Okay. Is there a last word you would like to say.

Bergmann: I will just say I love you.

Hall: I love you too. (laughs).

Postscript

PSYCHOANALYTIC WORK A DEUX

A patient:
I stutter falter and weave
between past and my present
wanting to leave
who is she to expect me to tell
the place that I live in is next to hell.

but as I continue
and keep coming back
I sense that she hears me
as I veer off track

at times I feel lost
what should I say
and the cost feels too high
but I know I can pay

new feelings surprise me
overwhelming at times
but I seem to recover
understanding my crimes

letting go of what haunts me
putting order to mess
the ghosts cease to taunt me
and sometimes caress

my mem'ries have softened
they had been so harsh
my reactions to others
are no longer brash

i stumble, tumble,
connect, deflect
she soothes, disrupts,
I muse, and connect
move ahead, fall back
aiming for balance.

i bumble, then brilliant
stumble, yet resilient
blind and seeing
this is kind of freeing
solve mysteries
review histories
concentrate
contemplate
learn
yearn
listen
laugh, cry, try,

it's hard to believe
all the things I'd forgotten
some of them great
some of them rotten

but i'm growing up
and it isn't so bad
I find myself smiling
no longer so sad

Analyst:
I listen and invite
her to tell me whatever
her pain and her fear
as we talk I'll hear

I mirror, disappear
engender trust and sometimes fear
to listen, tune out
stay calm, wanna shout
hide, collide, collude

take punishment
and adoration meant
for another
and very soon I recover

the dyad:
we rushed ahead and waited
felt the love
and we hated
charmed disarmed
caused alarm
and created

we wept, we laughed
sighed, frowned
argued
agreed
yes indeed.

we rejoiced
reacted
retracted
respected
and thru all those years
we felt protected

and now farewell
we both will grieve
our journey completed
well
spent
years

feel ready to end
it is time to part
but we'll always be
in each other's heart

Acknowledgements

I have been writing these riffs and essays for the past ten years and it's hard to remember everyone who encouraged me to publish them. So, in no particular order I thank many friends and colleagues.

My late friend Joann Turo listened to me talk these ideas through, both before and after a Cosmopolitan during our weekly dinners. Henry Kaminer's humor and agreement with many of my ideas gave me confidence. Ferne Traeger read chapters and her comments were spot on. Owen Renik, a jazz aficionado, took the time to listen to the listening chapter and read several others and his compliments mean so much to me. Arnie Richards' enthusiasm, praise, and belief in me over the years and for this book got me to the finish line. I chose IPBooks as publisher because of his encouragement and because of Tamar and Larry who I love dearly. Stewart Alter, a good friend, not in the field, gave me some excellent ideas regarding structure. Daisy Alter, who I've known since she was in kindergarten, asked good questions. Peter Dunn liked the mystery solving idea and his approval of my thoughts on the oedipus complex gave me courage. Wendy Olesker, who I hold in high esteem, gave a thumbs up on the masochism chapter. Henry Lothane, a true scholar was always available to answer questions about Freud. Matthew Bach, my official editor, knows his stuff and I thank him. Mark Poster, who I truly admire for his dedication to the future is the most well read person I know and was really helpful, and Barbara Stimmel, a fantastic writer, on a moments notice did wonders with the Self-Murder chapter. Karen Trokan was really enthusiastic about the listening chapter. Norman Doidge, a real inspiration, generously answered questions. Writing on the members list at ApsaA and sharing ideas helped because many people wrote to me privately and I made new friends. And thank you Stefano, Ric, Lance, Kerry M., and Aimee for the generous blurbs. Noel Moredo, type setter was great and Kathy Kovacic, who gave me ideas for the cover were both incredibly patient!

My daughter Devra, a professional writer has been wonderfully supportive, helpful, and always cheering me on. She agreed to be my copy-editor, taking time from her own work. And of course Jim Hall, though not here in body, is always with me in spirit. Most deserving of appreciation are the patients and all those who brought me their patients for supervision over these many years, allowing me to travel with them on journeys I shall never forget.

References

Ainsworth, M. S., Blehar, M. C., Waters, E., and Wall, S. (1978). *Patterns of attachment*. Hillsdale, N.J.: Lawrence Erlbaum.

Almond, R. and B. (1996). *The Therapeutic Narrative: Fictional Relationships and the Process of Psychological Change*. Westport & London, Praeger Publishing.

Balint, M. (1950). Changing Therapeutical Aims and Techniques in Psycho-Analysis. *International Journal of Psychoanalysis* 31:117–124.

Barron, J.W., Beaumont, R., Goldsmith, G.N., Good, M.I., Pyles, R L., Rizzuto, A. & Smith, H. F. (1991). Sigmund Freud: The Secrets of Nature and the Nature of Secrets. *International Review of Psychoanalysis* 18:143–163.

Beebe, B. & Lachmann, F. (2002). *Infant Research and Adult Treatment: Co-Constructing Interaction*. Hillsdale, NJ: Analytic Press.

Berliner, B. (1958). The Role of Object Relations in Moral Masochism. *Psychoanalytic Quarterly* 27:38–56.

Bion, W.R. (1962). *Learning from Experience*. London: Karnac Books.

Bird, B. (1972). Notes on Transference: Universal Phenomenon and Hardest Part of Analysis. *Journal of the American Psychoanalytic Association* 20:267-301.

Bowlby, J. (1940). Attachment and Loss. *International Journal of Psycho-Analysis*.

——— (1960). Grief and Mourning in Infancy and Early Childhood. *Psychoanalytic Study of the Child* 15:9-52.

Breger, L. (2009). *A Dream of Undying Fame: How Freud Betrayed His Mentor and Invented Psychoanalysis*. New York: Basic Books.

Bromberg, P. M. (1996). Standing in the Spaces: The Multiplicity Of Self And The Psychoanalytic Relationship. *Contemporary Psychoanalysis* 32:509-535.

Doidge, N. (2007). *The Brain That Changes Itself*. New York: Viking Books.

Doyle, A.C. (1894). *The Memoirs of Sherlock Holmes*. New York: Harper and Brothers.

Faimberg, H. (2005). *The Telescoping of Generations. Listening To the Narcissistic Links Between Generations*. London: The New Library of Psychoanalysis.

Fischer, N. (2019). *Nine Lives: Nine Case Histories Reflecting the Human Condition*. New York: IPBooks.

Fonagy, P. (2003). The development of psychopathology from infancy to adulthood: The mysterious unfolding of disturbance in time. *Infant Mental Health Journal* 24 (3):212–39.

Freud, S. (1912). Recommendations to Physicians Practising Psycho-Analysis. *Standard Edition*, 12:109–120.

——— (1914). *Remembering, Repeating, and Working Through. Standard Edition*, 12:145-156.

——— (1917). Mourning and Melancholia. *Standard Edition*, 14:237–258.

——— (1926). The Question of Lay Analysis. *Standard Edition*, 20:177–258.

Gay, P. (1988). *Freud: A Life For Our Time*. New York: W.W. Norton & Co.

Gibran, K. (1923). *The Profit*. New York: Alfred A. Knopf.

Gold, C.M., Tronick E. (2020). *The Power of Discord: Why the Ups and Downs of Relationships Are the Secret to Building Intimacy, Resilience, and Trust.* Boston: Little, Brown Spark.

Gorkin. M. (1984). Narcissistic Personality Disorder and Pathological Mourning. *Contemporary Psychoanalysis* 20:400–420.

Greenacre, P. (1956). Re-evaluaionof the process of working through. International ournal of Psycho-Analysis 37:439–444.

Greene, M.F. (2020). 30 Years Ago Romania Deprived Thousands of Babies of Human Contact. *The Atlantic* July/August. https://www.theatlantic.com/magazine/archive/2020/07/can-an-unloved-child-learn-to-love/612253

Grosz, S. (2013). *The Examined Life: How We Lose and Find Ourselves.* New York: W.W. Norton & Co.

Hall, J. (1998). *Deepening the Treatment.* Northvale, New Jersey, & London: Jason Aronson.

——— (2004). *Roadblocks on the Journey of Psychotherapy.* Northvale, New Jersey & London: Jason Aronson.

Hardin, H.T. & Hardin, D.H. (2000). On the Vicissitudes of Early Primary Surrogate Mothering II: Loss of the Surrogate Mother and Arrest of Mourning. *Journal of the American Psychoanalytic Association* 48:1229-1258.

Holtzman, D. & Kulish, N. (2000). The Femininization of the Female Oedipal Complex, Part I: A Reconsideration of the Significance of Separation Issues. *Journal of the American Psychoanalytic Association* 48:1413–1437.

Joffe, W. G. & Sandler, J. (1968). Comments on the Psychoanalytic Psychology of Adaptation, with Special Reference to the Role of Affects and the Representational World. *International Journal of Psychoanalysis* 49:445-454

Kantrowitz, J. (2020). *The Role of the Patient-Analyst Match in the Process and Outcome of Psychoanalysis.* New York: Routledge.

Karr-Morse, R. & Wiley, M.S. (1997). *Ghosts from the Nursery: Tracing The Roots of Violence.* New York: The Atlantic Monthly Press.

Knight, R. (2021). Reconsidering Development in Psychoanalysis, *The Psychoanalytic Study of the Child* 75:215-232.

Kohut, H. (1971). The *Analysis of the Self.* New York: International Universities Press.

Kris, E. (1956). The recovery of childhood memories in psychoanalysis. Psychoanalytic Study of the Child 11:54-88.

Kulish, N. (2002). Female Sexuality: The Pleasure of Secrets and The Secret Of Pleasure. *The Psychoanalytic Study of the Child,* 57:151–176.

Levine, R. (2016). *Stranger in the Mirror.* Boston: Little, Brown Spark.

Lee, P. (1946). *I Don't Know Enough About You. Santa Monica, CA: Universal Music-MGB Songs.* https://www.lyrics.com/lyric/1036832/Peggy+Lee/I+Don%27t+Know+Enough+About+You.

Lichtenstein, D. (1993). The Rhetoric of Improvisation Spontaneous Discourse in Jazz and Psychoanalysis. *American Imago* 50:227-252.

Lindner, R. (1982). *50 Minute Hour.* New Tork: Other Press.

Loewald, H. (1951). Ego and reality. *The International Journal of Psychoanalysis,* 32:10–18.

——— (1960). The Therapeutic Action of Psychoanalysis. *International Journal of Psychoanalysis* 41:16–33.

——— (1979). The Waning of the Oedipus Complex. *Journal of the American Psychoanalytic Association* 27:751-775

——— (1988). *Sublimation: Inquiries into Theoretical Psychoanalysis.* New Haven, CT: Yale Univ. Press.

Lothane, H. (2022). Personal Communication.

Main, M. (2000). The organized categories of infant, child, and adult attachment: Flexible Vs. Inflexible Attention under Attachment-Related Stress. *Journal of the American Psychoanalytic Association* 48 (4):1055–96.

Mills, J. (2005). *Treating Attachment Pathology.* Northvale, New Jersey & London: Jason Aronson.

McWilliams, N. (2011). *Psychoanalytic Diagnosis.* New York: The Guilford Press.

Morrison, T. (1987). *Beloved.* New York: Vintage International.

Nass, M. (1975). Personal Communication.

Ogden, T.H. (1994). The Analytic Third: Working with Intersubjective Clinical Facts. *International Journal of Psychoanalysis* 75:3–19.

——— (2004). The Analytic Third: Implications for Psychoanalytic Theory and Technique. *Psychoanalytic Quarterly* 73:167-195

——— (2007). Elements of analytic style: Bion's clinical seminars. *Int. J. Psychoanal.* 88: 1185–1200.

Orbach, S. (1999). *The Impossibility of Sex.* London & New York: Penguin Press.

Pankseep, J., Biven, L. (2012). *The Archeology of Mind: Neuroevolutionary Origins of Human Emotions.* New York & London: W.W. Norton & Company.

Piaget, Jean (1929). *The child's conception of the world.* London: Routledge & Kegan Paul.

Purcell, S. (2019). Psychic Song and Dance: Dissociation and Duets in the Analysis of Trauma. *The Psychoanalytic Quarterly* 88:2, 315-347.

Ramachandran, V.S. (2011). *The Tell-Tale Brain: A Neuroscientist's Quest for What Makes Us Human.* New York: W.W. Norton & Company.

Reik, T. (1933). New Ways in Psycho-Analytic Technique. *International Journal of Psychoanalysis* 14:321–334.

Rivers, J.
Ross, J. M. (1982). Oedipus Revisited—Laius and the "Laius Complex". *Psychoanalytic Study of the Child* 37:169-200.
Sandler, J. (1989). Guilt and Internal Object Relationships. *Bulletin of the Anna Freud Centre* 12(4):297–307.
——— (1990). On Internal Object Relations. *Journal of the American Psychoanalysis Association* 38:859–879.
——— & Rosenblatt, B. (1962) The Concept of the Representational World. *Psychoanalytic Study of the Child* 17:128-145
Shafer, R. (1994) *Retelling a Life*. New York: Basic Books.
Sharpe, E. (1950). *Collected Papers on Psychoanalysis.* London: Hogarth Press.
Shengold, L. (1989). *Soul Murder: The Effects of Childhood Abuse and Deprivation.* New Haven, CT: Yale University Press.
——— (1999). Soul Murder Revisited: Thoughts about Therapy, Hate, Love, and Memory. New Haven, CT: Yale University Press.
Schore, A. (2009). Attachment trauma and the developing right brain: Origins of pathological dissociation. In P. F. Dell & J. A. O'Neil (Eds.), *Dissociation and the dissociative disorders: DSM-V and beyond* (pp. 107–141). Routledge/Taylor & Francis Group.
Simon, B. (1991). Is the Oedipus Complex Still the Cornerstone of Psychoanalysis? Three Obstacles to Answering the Question. *Journal of the American Psychoanalytic Association* 39:641-668.
Solms, M. (2018). The neurobiological underpinnings of psychoanalytic theory and therapy. *Frontiers in Behavioral Neuroscience* 12 (294):1–13.
Solnit, R. (2014). Woolf's Darkness: Embracing The Inexplicable. *The New Yorker*, April 24.
Sripada, B. (2013). Email communication.

Spitz, R. (1945). Hospitalism: An Inquiry into the Genesis of Psychiatric Conditions in Early Childhood. *Psychoanalytic Study of the Child* 1: 53–74.

Stern, D. (1985). *The Interpersonal World of The Infant: A View From Psychoanalysis and Developmental Psychology*. New York. Basic Books.

Stone, L. (1954). The Widening Scope of Indications for Psychoanalysis. *Journal of the American Psychoanalytic Association* 2:567–594.

Tronick, E.Z., Process of Change Study Group, (1998). Dyadically expanded states of Consciousness and the Process of Therapeutic Change. *Infant Mental Health Journal* 19(3), 290–299.

——— (2001). Emotional connections and dyadic consciousness in infant-mother and patient-therapist interactions. *Psychoanalytic Dialogues* 11:187–194.

——— & Beeghly, M. (2011). Infants' Meaning-making and the Development of Mental Health Problems. *American Psychologist* 66(2):107–119.

Valenstein, A. (1973). On attachment to painful feelings and the negativer therapeutic reaction. *Psychoanalyic Study of the Child* 28:365-392 .

Winnicott, D.W. (1953). Transitional Objects and Transitional Phenomena—a Study of the First Not-me Possession. *International Journal of Psychoanalysis* 34:89–97.

www.ingramcontent.com/pod-product-compliance
Lightning Source LLC
Chambersburg PA
CBHW062122020426
42335CB00013B/1059
9781956864397